Comments on other *Amazing Stories* titles:

MW01045939

"Tightly written volumes filled with lots of wit and humour about famous and infamous Canadians."
Eric Shackleton, *The Globe and Mail*

"The heightened sense of drama and intrigue, combined with a good dose of human interest is what sets Amazing Stories *apart."*
Pamela Klaffke, *Calgary Herald*

"This is popular history as it should be... For this price, buy two and give one to a friend."
Terry Cook, a reader from Ottawa, on **Rebel Women**

"Glasner creates the moment of the explosion itself in graphic detail...she builds detail upon gruesome detail to create a convincingly authentic picture."
Peggy McKinnon, *The Sunday Herald*, on **The Halifax Explosion**

"It was wonderful...I found I could not put it down. I was sorry when it was completed."
Dorothy F. from Manitoba on **Marie-Anne Lagimodière**

"Stories are rich in description, and bristle with a clever, stylish realness."
Mark Weber, *Central Alberta Advisor*, on **Ghost Town Stories II**

"A compelling read. Bertin...has selected only the most intriguing tales, which she narrates with a wealth of detail."
Joyce Glasner, *New Brunswick Reader*, on **Strange Events**

"The resulting book is one readers will want to share with all the women in their lives."
Lynn Martel, *Rocky Mountain Outlook*, on **Women Explorers**

LETHAL LADIES

Crimes of Passion, Tales of Deceit and Treachery!

Cheryl MacDonald

CRIME/MYSTERY

James Lorimer & Company Ltd., Publishers
Toronto

James Lorimer & Company Ltd., Publishers acknowledge the support of the Ontario Arts Council. We acknowledge the financial support of the Government of Canada through the Canada Book Fund for our publishing activities. We acknowledge the support of the Canada Council for the Arts, which last year invested $20.1 million in writing and publishing throughout Canada. We acknowledge the support of the Government of Ontario through the Ontario Media Development Corporation's Ontario Book Initiative.

ONTARIO ARTS COUNCIL
CONSEIL DES ARTS DE L'ONTARIO

Canada Council
for the Arts

Library and Archives Canada Cataloguing in Publication

MacDonald, Cheryl, 1952-
Lethal ladies: crimes of passion, tales of deceit and treachery! / Cheryl MacDonald.

(Amazing stories)
Includes bibliographical references and index.
Issued also in an electronic format.
ISBN 978-1-55277-723-7

1. Women murderers–Canada–Biography.
2. Murder–Canada. I. Title. II. Series: Amazing stories (Toronto, Ont.)

HV6517.M35 2011   364.152'30820971   C2011-900770-3

James Lorimer & Company Ltd., Publishers
317 Adelaide Street West, Suite 1002
Toronto, Ontario, Canada
M5V 1P9
www.lorimer.ca

Printed and bound in Canada

Cover photo credit: Hamilton Public Library

FSC
www.fsc.org
MIX
Paper from
responsible sources
FSC® C016245

For Larry and Moira

Contents

Prologue

When the jurors shuffled back into the courtroom, every-one held their breath. It was 6:34 p.m. on September 13, 1946. Two days earlier, thirty-eight-year-old Elizabeth Popovich and her forty-eight-year-old husband had gone on trial at the Welland Courthouse, charged with murder and robbery of fifty-year-old Louis Nato. The jury had deliberated for just under two hours before returning to the courtroom. Now, in response to Justice W. Schroeder's question, they announced that they had found both defendants guilty of murder.

After briefly congratulating the jury, Justice Schroeder turned to the prisoners in the dock. "George Popovich and Elizabeth Popovich, stand up. Have you anything to say why sentence of the court should not be passed upon you?"

Without hesitation, George replied that he had two more witnesses. Elizabeth continued to protest her innocence. "I am not guilty and my husband is not guilty."

Schroeder ignored her plea, pointing out that they had both been found guilty. "I shall not say anything to you in this solemn moment, as that would only add to the anguish of your soul. The sentence of the court is that you shall be taken from the place in which you are confined and on

Tuesday, November 2, from thence you shall be taken to the place of execution and hanged by your neck until you are dead, and may God have mercy upon your souls."

Chapter 1
Grace Marks:
"My Misery Is Too Great for Words"

James Newton was mystified. It was Sunday morning, July 30, 1843, and, as he often did on a Sunday, he had stopped by to visit his good friend Thomas Kinnear. Only a day earlier he had seen Kinnear on Yonge Street, about three kilometres south of his Richmond Hill home. The men chatted briefly, with Newton promising to visit Kinnear later in the day, provided he got back from an athletic competition in Thornhill early enough. If not, he would definitely be there on Sunday.

Newton kept his word, but when he reached Kinnear's home, just a hundred metres off Yonge Street, there was no one in sight. Not his friend Thomas, nor Nancy Montgomery, the housekeeper who was also Kinnear's mistress, nor two younger servants, Grace Marks and James McDermott.

Newton knocked on the front door and when no one answered, went inside. The place was completely deserted.

Perplexed, he walked the half-kilometre to a cottage occupied by a man named Walsh, Kinnear's tenant. Walsh was not at home, but as he headed back to Kinnear's place, Newton met Walsh and explained the situation. Walsh returned with him and both men went back to Kinnear's, and entered the house.

This time, Newton walked from the front passageway into the kitchen, where he spotted bloodstains on the floor. Assuming one of the servants had killed a bird or two for dinner, Newton remained calm. But he was determined to discover what had happened to his friend and the rest of the household, so, leaving Walsh to watch the house, he headed over to Silas Wright's.

The Wrights were good friends of Nancy Montgomery, who had been expecting a baby when she started working for Kinnear, and who had chosen to give birth at the Wrights' house. When he was unable to find Nancy, or any information of Kinnear's whereabouts, he continued on to the house of another neighbour, the respected Francis Boyd, Esquire, and asked him to come back to the Kinnear farm.

By this time, Newton was growing concerned. In a

small, rural community like Richmond Hill, people kept a close eye on their neighbours. It seemed impossible that four people had vanished into thin air, literally overnight, without anyone knowing what had happened. Unable to rule out the possibility of foul play, Newton needed a respected, unimpeachable member of the community to witness what he had seen—and might yet see—at the Kinnear house.

As Newton and Boyd conducted a careful search, they realized that the house was "topsy-turvy," as though someone had rifled hastily through drawers and other storage areas. They found a closed book lying on Kinnear's bed, which had not been slept in. They searched other rooms, but found them empty. In the hall, they examined a carpet for traces of bloodstains, similar to those in the kitchen, but found none. Then they lifted the trap door that led from the passageway to the cellar.

Thomas Kinnear was lying on his back at the foot of the stairs, his left arm flung over his head, his feet about twenty-three centimetres apart. He had removed his boots, but otherwise was wearing the same clothes Newton had seen on him at their last meeting, on Saturday. This included a light jacket and a tartan vest, which were now stained with blood. He had been shot through the heart.

Boyd quickly sent word to David Bridgeford, one of the coroners for the Home District, who immediately conducted an inquest. His examination revealed that Kinnear had been shot at close range. The ammunition used was a lead ball, rather than a bullet, which had gone through the shoulder and broken the skin so that Kinnear bled onto the cellar floor. There was no blood on the stairs, suggesting the body had been dumped in the cellar almost immediately after death. But there was blood on the book which had been left on Kinnear's bed.

By this time, a gun had been found behind the pantry door in the kitchen. In addition, Newton was convinced that a number of valuable household items were missing, including some silver plate bearing the Kinnear family crest. It seemed a clear case of murder and robbery, and since the household servants were missing, they were the most logical suspects. Francis Boyd sent word to Alderman Gurnet, along with a description of Nancy, Grace and McDermott. Soon afterwards, a warrant was issued for all three.

Within a few hours, staff at Toronto's City Hall reported that a couple resembling Grace Marks and James McDermott had arrived in a horse-drawn wagon around five o'clock in the morning. After they had breakfast at the hotel, McDermott had gone out to get a shave, then returned. Before eight they were on their way again, headed for Toronto harbour. There, along with the horse and wagon, they boarded a steamer bound for Lewiston, New York.

The behaviour of the two young servants was highly suspicious. At the very least, it seemed they were guilty of stealing Kinnear's horse and wagon, and most likely they had committed murder. Yet, Toronto authorities refused to pursue them, arguing that the crime had been committed outside their jurisdiction, and they would not spend the money to immediately pursue the two most likely suspects.

This decision incensed Frederick Capreol, businessman and future railway developer who was a friend of Kinnear. Impulsively, he visited a Mr. Ogilvie and asked him for the loan of enough money to hire a steamboat. Ogilvie obliged. Capreol chartered the steamer *Transit*, and by one in the morning on Monday was on his way to Lewiston. Accompanying him was the high bailiff of Toronto, George Kingsmill, who was empowered to arrest Grace and McDermott, as well as a few other men.

The *Transit* made excellent time. By five o'clock in the morning it reached Lewiston. Kingsmill soon learned that Grace and McDermott had taken rooms at an inn close to the dock. He arrived to find that Grace was just getting dressed, while McDermott was asleep in an adjoining room. Putting Grace in the custody of one of his deputies, Kingsmill quietly entered McDermott's room and searched the pockets of his coat. He found keys and a gold snuffbox that was far too expensive to belong to a mere servant, as well as several other items that would subsequently be identified as Kinnear's. Then he woke McDermott.

Stalling for time, Kingsmill pretended to be a customs

officer and told McDermott if he had paid duty on the horse and wagon he could continue on his way. McDermott said he didn't have the cash, but would sell them the items and settle the matter. At that point, the man who was watching Grace called out from the bottom of the stairs, asking for instructions, and using Kingsmill's name.

McDermott, who had lived in Toronto for several months, realized who was confronting him. According to Kingsmill, he became "very agitated." He claimed he knew all about the crime and asked if there was any reward for Nancy. "If you find her you will know the whole secret, you may thank her for it all." McDermott also claimed that the horse and wagon, along with a number of other items, were his. Kingsmill thought otherwise, took him into custody and, along with Grace and all the personal items in the couple's possession, started back to Toronto.

Meanwhile, anticipating that Kingsmill would be successful in arresting Grace and McDermott and that they would be brought to trial, Francis Boyd, David Bridgeford and Robert Campbell had returned to the Kinnear house looking for additional clues. Part of their search focused on the basement, which was divided into two sections. Behind a partition were several barrels, and on close inspection, one of the men found an inverted tub from which a woman's legs protruded. When the tub was lifted, they found what was left of Nancy Montgomery. She had been hit in the head with an axe, then strangled. Although decomposition had begun, Coroner Bridgeford was able to ascertain that she was also pregnant.

The discovery of Nancy's body convinced investigators that Grace Marks and James McDermott had committed the crime. But there were formalities to be observed. After the arrested pair reached Toronto, they were taken to city hall and questioned separately.

Grace seemed an unlikely murder suspect. Just sixteen, she was of average height, slim and quite attractive, except for a rather long chin. Her hair was auburn, her eyes bright blue, and she had the fair, glowing complexion of an Irish farm girl. She was, she told interrogators, the third-eldest of nine children and had come to Canada with her parents in 1840. Since then, she had worked as a servant.

In June of 1843, she was staying with a shoemaker on Toronto's Lot Street. Nancy Montgomery visited from time to time, and offered her a position at a salary of $3 per week. When she arrived at Kinnear's house, she met James McDermott, who had been working there for about a week.

She soon realized that McDermott and Nancy did not get along. Nancy was forever scolding James, who finally complained to the master. Thomas Kinnear shrugged, telling James that Nancy was mistress of the house. That was not the answer McDermott wanted, but there seemed to be not much he could do about it. When Nancy told him his employment would be terminated as of July 28, he began plotting revenge.

Grace and James spent a lot of time together in the kitchen while Nancy sat with Kinnear in the parlour. Both employees resented Nancy's privileged position in the household and the condescending way she treated them. Before long, Grace said, James had formulated a plan. Knowing that the next time Kinnear went to the city he would likely return with a great deal of money, James decided to kill them both, take the money and leave. When he asked Grace to help him, she agreed.

It was Thursday, July 27, when Thomas Kinnear went into Toronto and Nancy informed McDermott that his employment was terminated, effective the next day. "Damn her," he swore, "Is that what she is at? I'll kill her before the morning." But the unexpected arrival of fourteen-year-old James Walsh delayed his plans. The son of Kinnear's tenant, the boy dropped by, bringing along his fife. With Kinnear away, Nancy thought it would be good to have a little fun, so she prevailed on young Walsh to play some tunes. Then, remembering that McDermott claimed to be a fine dancer, she asked him and Grace to dance. McDermott refused and was quite sulky throughout the afternoon and evening.

Around ten-thirty, Nancy picked up a candle to light her way to bed. McDermott walked outside, signalled for James Walsh to follow, then walked him home. When he returned, he told Grace he meant to kill Nancy with an axe while she slept in bed.

Grace was horrified. Whenever Kinnear was away the two women usually slept together, and she feared James might hit her instead. She persuaded him to wait until the next day. As Grace recalled it, James agreed reluctantly. "Damn her, I'll kill her then, the first thing in the morning."

Grace woke up early the next day, but when she got to the kitchen she found the fire already lighted and James cleaning shoes. He asked where Nancy was. Grace reported she was dressing and asked, "Are you going to kill her this morning?" McDermott said he was. "For God's sake," Grace pleaded, "don't kill her in the room, you'll make the floor all bloody."

Grace went out to the garden and returned to find McDermott cleaning knives in the kitchen. Then Nancy told her to make breakfast. At this point, McDermott was in the back kitchen, a sort of summer kitchen at the other end of the house that could only be reached by walking across the lawn. When Nancy told her to fetch some water from the pump in the yard, Grace walked outside. As she turned away from the pump, she saw McDermott dragging Nancy along the ground from the back kitchen to the front kitchen. He had smashed her head with an axe.

"I didn't think you were going to do it right away," Grace told McDermott. He replied that it was better to get it done, then asked if she would help, as she had promised, and open the trap door to the cellar. Grace told her questioners she refused—she was too frightened—and McDermott managed on his own. A little while later, he asked her for a handkerchief.

"What for?" Grace demanded.

"Never mind, she's not dead yet."

This time Grace followed him to the trap door in the passageway. As he climbed down into the cellar, she saw Nancy's body lying at the foot of the stairs. James told her to stay away and closed the trap door after him. A few minutes later, he emerged.

"Is she dead?" Grace asked.

"Yes," McDermott said, adding that he had put her body behind the barrels. And then he warned her that if she told anyone what she had witnessed her life would not be "worth a straw."

Grace protested, saying she could not help kill another woman, but would help do away with Kinnear. Satisfied, McDermott went to the kitchen to have breakfast. Grace followed, but could not eat.

When the meal was done, around ten o'clock, McDermott walked over to a nearby house, occupied by John Harvey, to borrow some gunpowder. John was not at home, but his mistress Hannah Upton was and she told McDermott he would have to ask John for what he wanted. McDermott ignored her, helped himself to the gunpowder, and walked back to Kinnear's.

Sometime that morning, Jonathan Jefferson, the local butcher, arrived at the house, as he usually did on a Saturday morning. He was surprised when Grace, rather than Nancy, met him at the kitchen door, and even more surprised when she said they did not need any meat that week.

Thomas Kinnear came home around eleven. After Grace removed various parcels from the wagon and took them into the house, McDermott took the horse and wagon into the stable. Almost immediately Kinnear asked for Nancy, and was told that she had gone into the city on the stage.

That was strange, Kinnear remarked, as he had met the stage on his journey homeward and had not seen her. Then he asked if there was any fresh meat in the house, expecting the butcher had already called. He had not, Grace told him, so Kinnear settled for eggs, tea and toast.

Following breakfast, he retired to his room and slept until early evening. When he awoke, he had his tea served in the dining room. Grace cleared the table, and while she was carrying the dishes into the front kitchen, McDermott told her he was going to kill Kinnear immediately. Grace continued about her business, carrying the tray to the back kitchen. That's when she heard a shot. Running to the front kitchen, she saw McDermott standing over Kinnear's body and the double-barrelled gun lying on the floor nearby.

Grace told authorities her first reaction was to run. She raced out the front door, heading towards the back kitchen. "Damn you!" McDermott shouted after her. Grace reached the door of the back kitchen and looked back to see McDermott standing on the lawn with a gun. Then he fired at her—and missed. The ball from the gun hit the jamb of the kitchen door.

Grace fainted. When she came to, a short time later, McDermott was bending over her. She asked why he had shot at her and McDermott told her he thought the gun was empty. Grace agreed to help him move Kinnear's body into the cellar.

Young James Walsh heard the shooting and came to investigate. McDermott told him he had been shooting at birds. But Walsh sensed something was not right. He noticed McDermott was wearing Kinnear's shoes and a straw hat that belonged to Nancy. And Grace was wearing white stockings and shoes, both of which were unusual for her.

Other things disturbed young Walsh. He knew that Kinnear owned both a horse and a colt. When he heard a chain rattling in the stable and asked about it, McDermott told him that the colt was unhappy because he was alone. Yet Walsh had never known the colt to be chained. And where was Nancy? Grace's response was peculiar. Laughingly, she said, "As if I would know so much!" Then she told Walsh a man had come to say that Mr. Silas Wright was ill and Nancy and the man had gone off on Kinnear's horse. What puzzled

James Walsh was that, if Kinnear was not at home, why would the horse have been there?

Wisely, he pretended to accept what he was told and turned to go home. McDermott escorted him part way across the lawn, then watched as he moved toward his own house. Satisfied that he was indeed leaving them, McDermott turned to Grace and told her that if James Walsh had gone into the house he would have killed him.

Over the next hour or so, Grace and McDermott rooted through drawers and cupboards, packing whatever took their fancy. At one point, they even went into the cellar. As Grace held a candle, McDermott searched Thomas Kinnear's pockets, removing his keys and his money. Then, under cover of darkness, they climbed into the wagon and set out for Toronto.

Grace claimed she had no choice but to accompany James McDermott, since he had already tried to shoot her once. Yet she waited for him at the hotel while he went to a barbershop to get a shave. She also agreed to marry him once they reached the United States. Still, she might have convinced people that she was totally innocent, except for McDermott's version of the story. According to him, she had been the first one to broach the subject of murder, suggesting that they poison Nancy. It had been Grace who strangled Nancy after McDermott had hit her with the axe. And, most telling of all, was that Grace had been wearing Nancy's clothing when she was arrested. If she had been an unwilling accomplice to double murder, would she not have felt uncomfortable in one of the victim's clothes?

James McDermott went on trial on November 4, was quickly found guilty and sentenced to death. Grace was also found guilty and sentenced to death, but, given her youth, the jury recommended mercy, and her sentence was commuted to life imprisonment. On Saturday, November 18, just before she was sent to prison in Kingston, she signed a confession in her jail cell. Three days later, James McDermott was hanged outside the Toronto jail.

Initially, Grace was a model prisoner: quiet, well-behaved, willing to work at whatever task was assigned her. But she was not happy. When her defence lawyer, Kenneth McKenzie, visited her in 1848, he found she still looked quite young, though not as pretty as she had been as a teenager. In addition, the "sullen assurance" that had been her typical facial expression had been replaced by a "sad and humbled expression." When McKenzie asked how she was, she told him, "My misery is too great for words to describe! I would gladly submit to the most painful death, if I thought that it would put an end to the pangs I daily endure."

In 1851, Grace began acting strangely. She would sing, laugh and chatter loudly and then fall into a depression. Every day she talked about seeing strange visions, and she slept badly. Doctors decided she was insane and sent her to the Provincial Lunatic Asylum, where she stayed for sixteen months before being returned to the penitentiary.

Susanna Moodie, who was acquainted with Grace's lawyer, visited her at the penitentiary and observed, "Grace Marks glances at you with a sidelong, stealthy look; her eyes never meet yours, and after a furtive regard, it invariably bends its gaze upon the ground." Moodie, an English gentle-woman who wrote extensively about her experiences in the "backwoods of Canada," included a melodramatic and partly fictionalized account of the murder and Grace's subsequent fate in an 1853 book, *Life in the Clearings Versus the Bush.*

According to Moodie, during her first eight years in prison Grace had behaved so well that she was allowed to work for the warden's family. Her good behaviour continued when she returned from the asylum, and in 1872 she was released. She immediately went to New York State and was never heard of again.

Chapter 2
Elizabeth Workman: "Have You Had Enough?"

Early on the morning of Thursday, October 24, 1872, Elizabeth Workman was scrubbing the floor in Samuel Butler's barbershop in Mooretown, not far from Sarnia. A Scottish immigrant who had come to Canada sixteen years earlier, Elizabeth had found neither happiness nor prosperity in her adopted country. Now in her early thirties, she had spent half her life in a miserable marriage, at the mercy of an abusive alcoholic husband who constantly harangued her. More than that, James was sometimes physically violent and Elizabeth had often been forced to seek shelter from his rages with neighbours.

Elizabeth Workman: "Have You Had Enough?"

Throughout their married life, Elizabeth had tried to do her best. She had raised Mary, James's daughter from an earlier marriage, as her own. She had cared for their son Hugh, now eight, making sure he was clothed, fed and attended school regularly. It had not been easy. James, who worked as a labourer, had rarely earned enough to bring even a modicum of comfort to the Workman household. Now that he was in his late fifties, the combined effects of alcohol and age were making it even more difficult for him to find and keep work.

Elizabeth had always done what she could to augment the family income, including taking in laundry or scrubbing floors. Sometimes it seemed completely futile. Like many men, James Workman considered anything his wife earned to belong to him. Whenever he needed money, he insisted Elizabeth turn her meagre wages over to him, and on at least one night had come home drunk, pulled her out of bed and bullied her into giving him all her cash.

But she would not give up. Mary, unable to bear her father's abusiveness any longer, had left the Workmans' place, was boarding with a Mrs. Skirving, and in fact, was now known around Mooretown as Mary Skirving. But Hugh was still too young to fend for himself, so Elizabeth kept doing what she could to support her little family.

That was why she was scrubbing the barbershop floor. Just a few weeks earlier, Samuel Butler, who had previously lived in Listowel, had moved to the Sarnia area. A single man who was somewhere around thirty-five or forty, he needed someone to clean his shop and do his laundry, and Elizabeth was happy to have the work. Samuel was pleasant company, sometimes visiting her and James at their bottom-floor flat and bringing along a bottle of whisky. But the camaraderie between them fuelled rumours in the small farming community. Gossips who knew Elizabeth was married to an abusive, ageing husband speculated that she was having an illicit affair with Samuel. That alone would have been bad enough in Victorian Ontario, but what really set tongues wagging was that Samuel Butler was black.

In 1793, Upper Canada was the first jurisdiction in the British Empire to enact legislation that would gradually phase out slavery. Although it did not immediately abolish that evil institution, the legislation introduced by the province's first lieutenant-governor, John Graves Simcoe, was seen as unusually progressive. But nothing could legislate against racism, especially when black settlement in Canada expanded in the wake of the American Fugitive Slave Act of 1850 and in the years leading up to the American Civil War. Although many Ontarians and other Canadians fought in the Union Army against the pro-slavery Confederates during that war, many continued to regard blacks as inferior. And even those who were willing to concede that, given the same opportunities, blacks could accomplish anything that whites could, drew the line at interracial relationships.

Inevitably, James Workman must have heard some of the gossip, and that October morning, after several drinks, he decided to do something about it. As Elizabeth worked on the barbershop floor, James suddenly appeared, pulling Hugh along beside him. Barging into the shop, he ordered Elizabeth to stop what she was doing and come home with him. When Elizabeth hesitated, he became more belligerent.

Samuel Butler was not prepared to tolerate this behaviour in his establishment. He quickly escorted Workman to the door, giving him a little push to make his point. Already unsteady because of the alcohol he had consumed, James stumbled and fell on some timber lying outside the barbershop. One labourer who was standing outside the shop later claimed he saw Samuel grab Workman's throat, pin the older man to the wall of the building and threaten him.

Whatever words were exchanged, Elizabeth decided there would be less trouble for everyone if she did what her husband asked and returned to their home. But she was angry, and when they reached their two-room flat, she unleashed the full force of her fury on her husband, beating him with a wooden mop handle. James spent the rest of the day in bed, sleeping off the combined effects of his drinking binge and the beating.

Samuel Butler came to their place after his work day was done, but this time he did not bring any whisky. Hugh, who slept in the dwelling's only bed with his parents, heard Samuel and Elizabeth talking long into the night. Around four in the morning, David Patterson, who lived in the upstairs flat, saw a man he later identified as Samuel leaving the Workman place. Patterson went back to bed, but when he woke up just before seven, he again saw Samuel leaving, this time carrying a bowl of pickles.

Whatever Patterson thought of what was going on, Hugh later stated that Samuel Butler had returned to drop off his laundry, and that the pickles he took away were a gift from Elizabeth. While Hugh went off to school and James remained in bed, Elizabeth started on her chores, including the laundry that Samuel had left. Then James woke up, and although he stayed in bed, he began harassing Elizabeth from the bedroom.

Upstairs, David Patterson's wife Sarah heard some of what was going on. James called to Elizabeth, insisting she come into the room, and scolding her because she had not left the barbershop when he told her to. He kept up his verbal abuse for hours. Finally, by mid-afternoon, Elizabeth had heard enough. She grabbed the mop handle, went into the bedroom, and started hitting her husband.

At some point—possibly earlier, while he was dozing, she had tied his legs so that he could not move from the bed. Now she began beating him, venting all her frustration she felt towards him. Sarah heard some of the blows as they landed on James's torso, arms and head. She also heard James shouting in pain, and Elizabeth asking, "Have you had enough? Have you had enough?"

Then Sarah heard an extremely loud blow. "I'm killed!" James screamed. The beating stopped, replaced by an ominous silence.

Soon afterward, Hugh returned from school. Elizabeth solemnly told her son that his father was seriously ill and might be dying. Then she filled a dish of pickles and carried it upstairs to Sarah Patterson. As they chatted, Elizabeth asked Sarah what she had heard from the Workman flat that afternoon. Sarah replied that she had heard the sound of someone being struck, as well as a lot of arguing. Rather than being upset, Elizabeth seemed pleased, telling her neighbour that she had given James a beating he would not forget any time soon, and that it might make her husband behave better in future. Sarah conceded that it just might do that.

That evening, Samuel Butler made another visit to the Workman residence. Again, he brought along a bottle of whisky, but this time he did not stay late into the night. He was gone before Hugh was sent to bed. No sooner had he left than James Workman resumed haranguing Elizabeth. But this time, Hugh noticed, his father's voice seemed weak.

James kept up his tirade as long as his strength would allow, then asked for a glass of water. Hugh brought it to him and helped him drink. Somewhat refreshed, James started berating Elizabeth once more. Unwilling to put up with the scolding, Elizabeth struck him on the shoulder with the mop handle.

The next day, Elizabeth apparently went about her usual household duties until early afternoon. Around two o'clock, she called David Patterson into the flat, saying, "Come and see what is the matter with father." Patterson crossed through the Workmans' kitchen, into the bedroom, took one look at James and sent Hugh upstairs to fetch Sarah. He then approached the bed, lifted James's head, and confirmed what he had suspected. James Workman was dead.

Sarah also took a close look at James. Both she and her husband noticed that his clothing seemed a little damp, as though he had been recently washed, and Sarah thought his body was rather stiff, as though he might have been dead for several hours. While Sarah stayed in the flat to keep Elizabeth company, David walked around the community, telling people that James Workman was dead.

At first, no one bothered to notify authorities. Instead, people who heard the news wandered over to the Workman place to pay their condolences and see the body for themselves. Mary Skirving was sent for, and she and Sarah Patterson tidied the small residence. As they did so, they disposed of the mop handle that Elizabeth had used to beat her husband.

Among the visitors who called was a merchant named

Brooks, who noted the livid bruises on James Workman's body and asked Elizabeth about them. "He got them by throwing himself about the room and hitting and abusing himself," she told him. Sarah Patterson and Hugh Workman both knew this was untrue, but thought that, possibly, Elizabeth's motive was to maintain some sense of dignity, rather than disclose the sordid details of her relationship with her husband. But she could not maintain that fiction for long.

On Saturday night, Dr. Edward Oliver and others arrived to begin the official investigation. One of the first things they did was to belatedly close the scene of James's death off to curious visitors. The following morning, Dr. Oliver conducted an autopsy. An examination of James's stomach indicated that he had not eaten for at least twenty-four hours prior to death. Oliver also found evidence of "twenty or thirty" bruises on his body, including a fatal blow near the left temple, which seemed to have been made by a "sharp cutting instrument." Looking around the small flat, he found two "butcher's tools" that seemed likely weapons.

Foul play was immediately suspected. On November 4, a coroner's jury determined that "James Workman came to his death by receiving excessive violence and from the evidence we believe that the said violence was inflicted by his wife, Mrs. Workman, or a Negro barber known as Samuel Butler, or both."

Elizabeth and Samuel were arrested. The rumours about their relationship suggested they might have conspired to kill James, but what also focused suspicion on Samuel was a remark he had made to a customer while Sarnia constable Robert Richmond was waiting in the shop. According to Richmond, Samuel had said that if James Workman didn't stay away from his premises, Samuel would "break his neck."

Although Elizabeth admitted to beating her husband, she claimed he had died of natural causes. She also insisted that Samuel had not been involved in any way. Nevertheless, both were kept in the Sarnia jail until the opening of the spring assizes on March 20.

As the trial got underway, it soon became apparent to authorities that Elizabeth had no lawyer, nor could she afford one. The court hastily appointed thirty-three-year-old John A. Mackenzie, a member of Sarnia Town Council, to defend her. Mackenzie was given until the next morning to review the case and come up with a defence.

The details of the case were well known to the community and there were no surprises at the trial. But Elizabeth's position was precarious, especially since Mackenzie did not call a single witness to testify in her defence. Instead, he relied on an emotional statement to the jury, emphasizing the abuse James had heaped on her and that those who knew her regarded her as a hard-working, dutiful wife.

Whatever sympathy Mackenzie might have inspired in

the jury, it was undermined by the judge's closing statement. Scottish-born Adam Wilson was fifty-nine, a seasoned politician who had served two terms as mayor of Toronto, and a respected legal mind who would later be knighted.

He advised the jury that there was nowhere near enough evidence to convict Samuel Butler. But Elizabeth was another case entirely. She was, Judge Wilson said, "not very kind to her husband" and he had heard no evidence that her husband had ever physically abused her. In addition, Butler had taken Elizabeth's side against her husband and threatened James with bodily harm, which, in his opinion, "pointed to some kind of improper intimacy." In addition, the circumstantial evidence was compelling. She had been seen leaving the bedroom where James had been tied and beaten, she had admitted beating him, did not send for a doctor when it seemed his condition was deteriorating and had delayed notification of the proper authorities. The jury, Wilson said, had no choice but to find Elizabeth Workman guilty of murder.

The jury accepted the judge's direction, although they strongly recommended mercy. Elizabeth was sentenced to be hanged on June 19, 1873.

Juries in this period often recommended mercy when there were mitigating circumstances. Many people believed Elizabeth's statement that she had not meant to kill James, even if she did admit to beating him. In addition, there were the repeated reports of James's repeated abuse. Although Judge Wilson said there was no evidence that this was physical, Elizabeth had frequently gone to neighbours when James became too violent. Officially, the governor general was empowered to commute a death sentence to a prison term. In practice, he followed the recommendation of the minister of justice, who, at this time, was also the Canadian prime minister, Sir John A. Macdonald. A lawyer himself, Macdonald relied on the opinion of the presiding judge in making his decision, and Wilson saw no reason to honour the jury's recommendation. "The fact remains that she did commit the acts charged to her and she alone," Wilson wrote in a letter to Macdonald. He also stressed that the Workmans "were of a very low class," an opinion that was strengthened by Elizabeth's suspected relationship with a black man, Samuel Butler.

Meanwhile, encouraged by the *Sarnia Observer*, petitions began to circulate asking for commutation of Elizabeth's death sentence. Five different petitions were signed by a total of 628 people, including the Crown attorney who had prosecuted her. The constant theme was that Elizabeth was a "sober, industrious woman of good character who worked hard to support her husband and child though often deprived by her husband of her hard earnings as soon as obtained" and that James "was very dissipated and cruel and frequently ill-treated her." MP and future prime minister

Alexander Mackenzie also added his voice to those begging for mercy for Elizabeth although, in a letter to the prime minister dated May 18, he expressed no surprise at Wilson's view on the case, given that nothing had been done to bring out Elizabeth's side of the story.

The *Observer* also pointed out that others recently convicted of murder, including a man who had shot another in cold blood, had escaped the gallows. But Elizabeth would not. In spite of a last-ditch effort by Sarnia council to present a petition to the governor general in person, no clemency was forthcoming.

In mid-June, the gallows was erected in the yard of the Sarnia jail. Executions were no longer carried out in front of the jail, as they had once been, but interested members of the public were still permitted to witness the final step in the process of justice. Public opinion was so strongly opposed to Elizabeth's execution though, that only fifteen or sixteen people, aside from the required court officials, attended.

In the months since her trial, local clergymen and charitably inclined ladies had frequently visited her to bring what spiritual and emotional comfort they could. Elizabeth had been raised a Presbyterian, and took considerable comfort from ministrations of the local Presbyterian minister, the Reverend John Thompson. He told the newspaper that Elizabeth was very grateful for the kindness she had received, especially from Mrs. Allen, the matron of the jail. He also stated that she had forgiven the people whose testimony had helped convict her.

Hours before the execution, Thompson and some other ministers gathered in Elizabeth's cell, reading scripture and singing psalms. When the time came, she remained composed, much more so than Thompson, climbing the steps to the gallows steadily and with little hesitation.

In one hand she clutched a white handkerchief and a bouquet of flowers.

Elizabeth recited the Twenty-third Psalm along with Thompson. As she was placed on the trap door, she addressed the spectators, saying that she hoped her story would be a lesson to "wives who have drunken husbands and husbands who have drunken wives." Moments later, she dropped seven feet, dying instantly.

For twenty minutes, her body hung from the gallows, the handkerchief and flowers still clutched in her hand. Then she was laid gently in the coffin that had been waiting nearby. The handkerchief and flowers were placed on her breast, the lid closed and the coffin buried under the gallows.

It would be twenty-six years before another woman convicted of murder in Canada paid with her life. Elizabeth Workman is still the only Canadian woman to have been executed in spite of a jury's recommendation for mercy.

Chapter 3
Eleanor Navin: "Good Lord, Ed Is Dead!"

The knock came at one a.m. on Saturday, November 20, 1880. Through his closed door, Thomas Wiskin heard a neighbour, Eleanor Navin, shout, "Good Lord, Ed is dead!"

Just that afternoon Wiskin had seen Edward Navin walking home, two or three paper-wrapped parcels in his arms. He seemed perfectly sober and in good health. Knowing that Eleanor was overly fond of whisky, Wiskin assumed she was drunk and at first did not answer the knock, but reconsidered after a few moments. He opened the door to see Eleanor leaving. Then she turned to speak to him and fell to the ground. Alexander, her young son, helped her up as Wiskin asked how Ed had died.

"I don't know," she replied.

Wiskin shrugged and let her continue on her way home.

At first light the following morning, Eleanor called on Mary Hamm, who, with her husband Fred, owned the farm on which the Navins' rented house was located. Eleanor told Mary that her husband had fallen and killed himself, and that she wanted William Hamm to help move the body. Mary thought that was a bad idea and told Eleanor to go to another neighbour.

James Galt was in the barn when Eleanor found him. She explained that her husband had fallen on an axe and killed himself, and she needed someone to move the body. Galt rounded up some other men, Allen Omey, George Daley and W. C. Scott, and walked over to the Navin house.

It was little more than a hut, about five and a half metres long and just over three and a half wide. Upstairs, the Hamms stored various items, accessible from an outside door. On the ground floor, a single door from the outside led to a small, low-ceilinged room. Galt, who had known the Navins for about ten months, was the first one to go inside. Edward Navin was lying on his back, his head towards the door, one foot under the damper of the stove. There was a cut on one side of his head.

Galt noted blood on the floor, and also streaks that indicated someone, probably Eleanor, had cleaned up quite a bit of it. Galt also noticed there was sawdust on the floor, and that the ceiling was so low that anyone swinging an axe was likely to hit it.

Eleanor's story, which she would repeat several times over the next few days, was that she had gone to Bath on Friday and returned home by half past two. She and Edward spent the rest of the afternoon drinking and had dinner at four. After dark, Edward had sent her to Bath for another bottle of whisky, which she purchased from hotelkeeper David McBride. When she got home around ten, she found the house dark, the stove gone cold and Edward in bed.

When Eleanor asked her husband to get up and make a fire he sent her for a cedar fencepost to cut up for firewood. After he tried, unsuccessfully, to shave off some thin pieces for kindling, Eleanor started sawing the post. That's when Edward told her, "Find me that axe and I will split it." According to Eleanor, it was around eleven-thirty when Edward got the axe. At that point, he told her to go fetch more wood. Before she returned, one of her boys called out that Edward had fallen. When Eleanor re-entered the house, she found her husband lying on the floor in a pool of blood and the axe beside him.

She went to see Tom Wiskin, who, she claimed, did not answer his door. Then she returned to her own place, wiped up some of the blood and waited until morning.

Word quickly got around, bringing the usual curiosity

seekers and a local newspaper reporter, Robert L. Henry. According to Henry, Eleanor thought Edward had fallen on the axe and killed himself, but after sorting out the details, Henry came to the conclusion that the man had hit the ceiling as he swung the axe and it had then hit him in the head. But, like some of the other men who entered the house that day, Henry looked at the low ceiling for marks of an axe, and found none.

Authorities were notified. The first to examine the body was Dr. Kennedy, who said that Edward was still warm. To him, this suggested that he might have been in a coma during part of the time that Eleanor thought he was dead. He also found that his skull was fractured, but his opinion was that the injury would most likely have been caused by a fall, rather than an axe.

Dr. Bristol conducted the post-mortem in the Navin house and discovered three wounds. One was a cut on Edward's forehead, about two inches above his left eye, a minor injury that would not have caused death. But further examination showed that his skull had been fractured by a "massive blow" from a blunt instrument. As far as Bristol was concerned, Edward could not have hit himself in the head with such force.

A coroner's inquest was scheduled for Monday. In the meantime, Eleanor had to make arrangements for her husband's burial. She had no money to purchase a coffin or hire an undertaker, so some of the men in the neighbourhood put together a rough coffin made of boards removed from nearby fences. Some of the boards were painted with advertisements. Edward was lowered into the crude casket, along with the top of his skull, which had been removed during the autopsy, and put into a shallow grave on the south side of the local Lutheran cemetery.

When the coroner's inquest began, much of the questioning centred on the characters of Eleanor and Edward Navin. Witness after witness testified that Edward had been a harmless individual—"quiet" and "inoffensive" in the opinion of William Smith. Some said they had never seen him drunk. Others admitted that he did drink from time to time, but not excessively. Dr. Kennedy, one of the doctors who had examined Edward's body, told another story, however, saying that Edward had been addicted to alcohol and that his reputation was only "fair."

The witnesses' opinion of Eleanor was another matter altogether. William Smith, Eleanor's son-in-law, testified that, a couple of months before Edward's death, he had seen Eleanor knock him down with a wooden bar from the door, hitting him near the temple and the eye. A few weeks later, Smith was at the Navin house when Eleanor's brother was visiting. According to Smith, the two of them told Edward to get out, threatening to kill him if he didn't leave. Smith also claimed that one time when she was drinking Eleanor had gone to a drawer, pulled out a butcher knife and threatened to have her husband's "heart's blood." Smith's wife had pushed Eleanor back into a chair.

John Stuart, who had occasionally visited the Navins and also sometimes slept in the storage area on the second floor of the building, also told of Eleanor's abusiveness. She used "very violent language" towards him, and according to a story Edward had told him, Eleanor had knocked him down twice "until he rolled like a pumpkin." He said visitors were constantly calling at the house at all hours, often drunk, and often using vulgar language. Stuart's testimony more or less paralleled what Smith had said—and that he too had left the house after being threatened.

The coroner's jury concluded that Edward had died "as a result of injuries inflicted by the hand of his wife, Eleanor Navin." Eleanor was sent to Napanee jail to await the spring assizes and her trial for murder.

The proceedings got underway on April 21, 1881, amid rumours that dogs had dug up Edward's shallow grave and devoured his body. In fact, some medical students had exhumed the corpse a short time after burial and taken Edward's remains to the medical school at Queen's University in nearby Kingston, where it remained as an anatomical specimen.

Because she was destitute, Eleanor was defended free of charge by a Mr. Madden. Robert Henry covered the trial, and noted that she appeared calm when first brought into the courtroom, but burst into tears when arraigned. She quickly regained her composure, however, and when asked how she pleaded, answered "Not guilty," in a "clear, audible voice."

Eleanor seemed calm at first, but more and more anxious as she looked around the court and absorbed the solemnity of the occasion. Henry was impressed by the dramatic change in her appearance since she had been sent to jail. "Instead of the grimy pallor of her sunken face bearing the traces of a recent debauch that ended in the death of her husband, her face looked plump and healthy, and in the place of the slatternly garments which hung on her gaunt figure, she wore a neat black dress, covered by a plain woollen shawl." The dress was alpaca, trimmed with a little lace at the neck and complemented by an old gold-coloured brooch. Eleanor also wore a black straw hat trimmed with black satin and ostrich feathers, sky-blue stockings and slippers.

While she had taken some trouble about her appearance, she could not hide her anxiety. According to Henry, "Her eyes glanced furtively from side to side, and the working of the muscles of the jaw betrayed the grating of her teeth, an exercise which she kept up uninterruptedly all day."

Although a number of witnesses were called, what would have been two of the most important had made themselves scarce. John Stuart had left the area in search of work, and William Smith, Eleanor's son-in-law, had apparently decided he would not repeat the stories of Eleanor's abusive behaviour if her life hung in the balance. Their absence weakened B. M. Britton's case against her, but he made up for the dearth of witnesses with an opening address that painted a vivid picture of disgraceful behaviour in the Navin household, not only because of the drinking and the alleged murder, but also because Eleanor's young children were left alone with their father's corpse during the night, and because of the shoddy manner in which the body was eventually interred.

Eleanor sat stoically through it all, her jaw working, but hung her head when Britton described the wounds found on Edward's body.

Among the witnesses called to the stand was Alexander Navin, who had accompanied his mother to the neighbours' on the fateful night. He was about eleven, and, according to Henry, appeared quite intelligent. The judge questioned him closely about the importance of telling the truth. While Alexander replied that he understood that little boys who told lies "went to a bad place," with a little more probing the judge discovered that he had not been told much about right and wrong by his natural parents, but had only recently learned these lessons from Mrs. Leslie, his foster mother. Citing "religious ignorance," the judge declared Alexander would not make a competent witness.

Most of the witnesses called reiterated testimony that

had been given at the inquiry. Among them was David Franklin, who had known Eleanor since she was a girl. Once, during a quarrel when they had both been drinking, he had heard Eleanor call her husband a liar. When Edward responded by slapping her, Eleanor seized the wooden bar used to close the door and hit him in the head. Then they both shook hands and "made friends."

The defence rested his case on expert testimony from various doctors associated with the medical school in Kingston. Dr. Michael Sullivan had seen Edward's remains there and stated, "I never before saw a skull so extraordinarily thin." Four other expert witnesses said basically the same thing, agreeing that, under the circumstances, a blow from an axe should have made a much larger fracture, and that Edward's injury was more consistent with falling against the corner of a stove. They also presented the theory that the first men on the scene had discussed, that Edward had lifted the axe overhead to split wood, grazed the low ceiling of the room with it, lost control of the axe and hit himself in the back of the head.

The judge advised the jury they could bring in a verdict of either murder or manslaughter, but enough confusion had been raised through the medical testimony for them to take another route. At 6:15 p.m., after about fifteen minutes of deliberation, the jury foreman declared Eleanor Navin not guilty.

The judge seemed pleased with the jury's decision. Addressing Eleanor, he "strongly cautioned her," urging her to stop drinking, since it had not only made her a widow but had nearly cost her her life. Eleanor seemed to barely be listening—she was so excited about the verdict. As soon as she was set free, she headed for home on what is now Highway 2.

After five months of sobriety in the shadow of the gallows, Eleanor might well have taken the opportunity to turn her life around. Whether she tried and failed is not recorded, but she eventually returned to her old habits. Along the way she produced at least one more child. In 1896 she was arrested in Napanee for drunkenness and for threatening to throw her daughter into the Maitland River. John Carson, who was both mayor of the town and a police magistrate, dismissed the charges because putting Eleanor in jail would have meant extra hardship for the little girl, but told Eleanor she was only free to go if she left town. Probably recalling the months she had spent in the local jail, she took Carson's advice and headed for parts unknown.

Chapter 4
Florence Kinrade: "I See the Man!"

On February 25, 1909, the quiet gentility of Hamilton's Herkimer Street was shattered by a gruesome murder. Around four in the afternoon, twenty-three-year-old Florence Kinrade raced across from her parents' gracious Victorian brick house to the home of a neighbour, Mrs. Frank Hickey. "Ethel is shot! Shot six times!" she screamed, then fell to the floor.

Mrs. Hickey told Florence to stay in the house while she alerted the police. Instead, the young woman ran to a nearby grocery store owned by George Hunt. After Hunt called the police, he and a clerk, D. M. Brown, each grabbed long butcher knives and cleavers and raced to the Kinrade house. They found twenty-four-year-old Ethel lying in a pool of blood at the bottom of a narrow flight of stairs leading to the dining room. Still wearing her hat, she was dressed in street clothes, her shirtwaist ripped and singed by four bullets discharged at close range. She had also been shot just in front of the left ear. The dark stains of gunpowder on the young woman's cheek indicated that the muzzle of the gun had been pressed close to her face.

Police received the report at 4:03. Within ten minutes, Detective Bleakeley and Constable Burch arrived in a patrol wagon. The coroner, Dr. McNichol, also reached the scene quickly. McNichol, who also lived on Herkimer Street, had been about to set out on his rounds when the police summoned him. After briefly examining Ethel's body, he concluded that she had probably died instantly—and that she had been dead for some time.

Across the street, Florence had collapsed on Mrs. Hickey's couch. It took some time before the coroner and the police were able to get any semblance of a coherent story out of her, but eventually she calmed down enough to tell them what had happened.

A tramp had come to the door, asking for something to eat. But once he got into the foyer of the house, he demanded money and valuables. Knowing that she and her sister were alone in the house, Florence shouted to Ethel to lock herself in her room, then climbed the stairs to get money for the intruder. As she was returning to the ground floor, she heard a shot coming from the dining room, then five more shots.

Florence ran into the dining room, gave the money to the tramp, and then escaped into the backyard. At one time, there had been an opening in the fence that surrounded the yard, but recently it had been closed up, while Florence was away from Hamilton. In her panic, she had apparently forgotten this. So she went back into the house, to find the murderer still in the dining room.

"He told me that if I squealed he would shoot me too," she recalled. Nevertheless, she tried to grab the revolver from him before running to a front window. Too frightened to call for help, she raced from the house to get help from Mrs. Hickey.

Once the men arrived and she had regained some degree of composure, Florence was able to provide a description of her sister's killer. He was around thirty-five years old, five feet six inches or five feet seven inches tall, rather stout, with a dark complexion and a flowing dark moustache that hid his mouth. He was dressed a little better than the average transient, but not quite as nicely as a gentleman, in a dark suit and overcoat. He also wore a soft felt hat, pulled low over his face, but Florence was still able to discern a "wild stare" in his eyes.

Tramps were a problem in most North American cities

and large towns in the late nineteenth and early twentieth centuries. Many jobs, especially those involving manual work and minimal skills, were seasonal. Unemployment soared during winter months. With no employment insurance and no reliable welfare system to fall back upon, job-hunters drifted from place to place, taking whatever temporary work they could find. Municipal governments considered them a perpetual problem, and Hamilton had been wrestling with the issue of unemployed transients for some time. According to a 1909 newspaper report, "This city is the softest place they ever struck." Not only did vagabonds head to Hamilton in large numbers, they also spread the word about which people in the small city were most "charitably inclined" and made a point of calling on them.

The Kinrade family reputedly fit that description, or at least Thomas Kinrade, Florence and Ethel's father, did. In 1909, Kinrade was principal of the Cannon Street school, and also the owner of about thirty rental properties. Because he had done so well, he felt it was his Christian duty to help the less fortunate. He gave instructions to his family to answer the door when tramps came calling and to give them what they needed. Sometimes it was simply a matter of something to eat, but more often the Kinrades signed lodging tickets. Presented at boarding houses, these allowed the tramps to obtain food and shelter, which were then charged to Thomas Kinrade.

Florence Kinrade: "I See the Man!"

Unfortunately, Christian charity had its drawbacks. Some transients were drawn to the "fashionable residential district" where the Kinrades lived. While most were probably content to get some food or a lodging ticket, others lingered in the area and caused some problems. In fact, one of the reasons Ethel and Florence were alone in the house was that their mother had gone downtown to complain about a tramp that had been lurking in the neighbourhood.

As she was returning from her visit to the police station, Bella Kinrade spotted the police patrol wagon parked outside her house. Earl, a married son living in Montreal, had recently been ill, and when Mrs. Kinrade saw the wagon she mistook it for a hearse and jumped to the conclusion that her son had died. Mrs. Hickey had been keeping an eye out for her neighbour and called to Bella to come across the street to her house. She started out, but, overcome by the shock of what she believed to be her child's death, fainted as she neared the Hickey house. Fortunately, a man passing by caught her before she hit the ground and helped her inside.

Someone also called Thomas Kinrade at school to tell him his daughter had been killed, but apparently did not say whether it was Ethel, Florence, or sixteen-year-old Gertrude. When he reached home, he was kept waiting a few minutes, then allowed into the dining room. The body was on a stretcher, covered with a waterproof cloth. As Thomas approached it, he muttered, "I've suspected something like

53

this would happen." He gently pulled aside the waterproof covering and looked down at his dead daughter's face.

A Hamilton newspaper described what happened next in typically melodramatic terms.

"Oh, which of my girls is it? Is it you, Florence? No. It is not you. My God, my God! It is Ethel! Oh, what coward could have done this? Why did he not shoot me? Oh, I would have given my life for my poor, poor girl!" After pulling himself together, he went across the street to Mrs. Hickey's to talk to Florence, then took her back home for a half-hour interview with detectives.

Meanwhile, via the call boxes interspersed along the city streets, Hamilton police were ordered to keep an eye out for anyone matching the description Florence had provided. But the tramp seemed to have vanished into thin air.

After police had interviewed Florence and scoured the property for any signs of physical evidence, Ethel's body was taken to Hamilton City Hospital and placed in the morgue. Constable Robert Lentz rounded up fifteen men to form a coroner's jury, and at eight thirty that evening they gathered at the morgue to examine the corpse. Ethel was still fully clothed, still wearing her hat. After examining her wounds, and ascertaining that they had been caused by bullets that were .38 calibre or possibly something larger, the men recommended an autopsy, set an inquest date for Wednesday, March 3, and adjourned.

Florence Kinrade: "I See the Man!"

In almost no time, word spread throughout Hamilton and beyond. Newspapers carried the story of the murder in a respectable middle class home. Everyone seemed to be speculating about what had happened, and police stations and newspaper offices were flooded with reports that the suspected perpetrator had been spotted. According to one rumour, he was seen on a Hamilton streetcar, anxious and impatient, on his way to a local train station. Someone claimed to have seen him on Charlton Avenue, someone else on South James Street, another person on Markland Street. In Buffalo, a man resembling Florence's description of the murderer was arrested, but released after a day in jail. Meanwhile, stories circulated about close encounters with tramps in the area of the Kinrade house. One report told how three young women were walking home on the night before the murder. A short distance from their homes, they separated. One of the trio claimed she saw a tramp hanging about the Kinrade place. Although the girl was very athletic, there was something about that man that was so disturbing that she drew a large hatpin out of her hat, preparing to defend herself. Another report said respectable women had seen a tramp hanging around alleys near Herkimer Street and that he had "shocked them with his actions."

The most disturbing accounts came from the Kinrade family themselves. From around the middle of February, they said, a man had been hanging about their property. Both Ethel and Florence had reported seeing him on the verandah, and, on one occasion, he had pressed his face against the window of the front door of the house and peered in. Bella Kinrade relayed these incidents to the police on the afternoon Ethel was killed, and also told them that someone tried to open a window from the verandah a few nights before the murder.

But, as the investigation continued, various questions arose. One puzzling aspect was how Florence had escaped with her life. It was speculated that the intruder had fired all the bullets in his revolver when he shot Ethel, but he still had the gun in his hand while Florence was in the house. Presumably the man was stronger than the slender twenty-three-year-old, who was the only person who could put him at the scene of the crime, yet Florence had managed to get away from him—twice.

Equally puzzling was why he had lingered in the Kinrade house after killing Ethel. Some thought that the man must be insane, and for a time there was a rumour that he had escaped from the Hamilton mental hospital, located a short distance away on the Niagara escarpment. But no one had escaped on the day in question, and all the patients who were allowed out on passes were accounted for.

Most puzzling of all was where the intruder had gone after leaving the Kinrade house. It was only a matter of minutes between the time Florence gave the alarm and when the men rushed into the Kinrade house. It was still light out, and

Herkimer Street and the surrounding area were compara-
tively well travelled by both pedestrians and vehicles. Yet the
intruder seemed to have vanished without a trace.

To some extent, the investigation was hampered by
the mental conditions of both Florence and her mother.
Newspapers reported them both to be in "serious" condition, suffering from hysteria and nerves. According to one
of her sons, Mrs. Kinrade had a history of nervous disorders
and frequently fainted when overwrought. Florence, who
was described by her father as "of a lively nature," was made
of stronger stuff; yet she, too, seemed almost unhinged by
the trauma of her sister's murder. Just the same, detectives
repeatedly questioned her, stopping only when she fainted
or broke down in tears.

Their persistence brought out inconsistencies in
Florence's story. In one version, she said that she and Ethel
were both upstairs when the man came into the house.
Florence went part way down the dining room stairs and
confronted him. The intruder told her he wanted money and
threatened to shoot her if she screamed. Florence shouted to
Ethel to lock herself into her room, but, instead of comply-
ing, Ethel raced down the stairs. As Florence handed him
$10 with which she had planned to go shopping, Ethel said
something and the intruder menaced her with the revolver.
Unable to control herself, Ethel either spoke or screamed and
the tramp opened fire.

Florence also told her father that she might have fainted at some point. At the inquest, Thomas Kinrade testified that his daughter had told him that, once she had given the $10 to the tramp, she had tried to climb out the back parlour window in the back parlour. The man dragged her back into the room, an act that was a shocking violation of Edwardian propriety. "I can feel his hands on me yet, Father," Florence told Thomas.

Initially, investigators assumed the discrepancies in Florence's various accounts of events were a result of the trauma she had experienced. But gradually they came to the conclusion that something was seriously amiss with the stories. Soon, Ontario Provincial Detective John Miller, who had been called in to investigate, was telling reporters that the "tramp theory" was not particularly strong.

Hamilton's mayor John Inglis McClaren said basically the same thing the day after the murder when the city council posted a $500 reward for the arrest of the murderer. "The people have no need to be alarmed about tramps," he told reporters. "This crime was not committed by any tramp or burglar. No, I don't think the police are looking for any tramp."

It might have been a political move on McClaren's part, calculated to set Hamiltonians' minds at ease. But Florence's vagueness on some details, such as the colour of the intruder's hair and moustache, suggested that the tramp might have been a figment of her imagination. Or possibly she was hiding something, perhaps in an attempt to protect someone known to her. Furthermore, based on the accounts of various people who had been near the Kinrade home, there was a huge discrepancy in the timing of events. A streetcar driver revealed that he had seen a young woman rushing out of the Kinrade house and over to the Hickey residence at 3:25 p.m., which would have put the time of the shooting around 3:15— nearly forty-five minutes earlier than Florence had claimed!

Police explored different possibilities. Was there a man in Ethel's life, a jilted or jealous suitor, who had killed her in a fit of passion? Did she or her father have personal enemies? Not as far as any family members were aware, they were told. Then what of problems within the family? Were the Kinrades on good terms with one another? According to their testimony at the inquest, they were. But the investigation revealed some disturbing information about Florence.

The young woman was known in Hamilton for her beautiful soprano voice and had been a soloist in a local church, as well as a special guest at various churches around southern Ontario. In 1908, she had travelled to the southern United States at the invitation of an acquaintance in order to sing in a church choir there. Florence provided some details about her experiences, but many of them could not be corroborated. What investigators did discover, the inquest was told, was that, against the wishes of her father, she had been a vaudeville performer, singing and acting in comic skits in Virginia and Georgia.

Singing in church was one thing. Singing and cavorting in a theatre was quite another, and still considered not entirely respectable, especially for well brought up young women like Florence. But there was more. Although Florence emphatically denied it, one of her brothers testified that it was his impression that she had learned to use a gun in order to protect herself from the unwanted attentions of her male admirers and other individuals she might encounter during her show business career.

Finally, detectives turned up a young man named Jimmie Baum, a southern playwright and actor who had co-starred with Florence in vaudeville performances. According to Jimmie, Florence claimed her parents had forced her to marry an older man against her will, but she had divorced him. Jimmie described how Florence had, without his knowledge, replaced a knife in one of their comedy sketches with a gun loaded with blanks. He also revealed that he and Florence had been engaged. Questioned about this at the inquest, Florence replied that it had been just a joke. Reporters covering the proceedings watched Jimmie's expression as she spoke and saw his face go scarlet. He later told reporters that he thought her family had persuaded her to make light of the engagement.

Although Florence had broken off her relationship with

Jimmie just two weeks before her sister's murder, at the time of Ethel's death she was already engaged to another man. Clair Montrose Wright, the son of a Methodist minister, was a graduate of Victoria College and a Methodist minister in training. During the weeks following the murder, he was frequently seen with Florence, often supporting her when she seemed about to collapse, and sometimes going even further than that. Florence repeatedly "swooned" during the investigation and the inquest whenever the questioning became too stressful. Sometimes, in her semi-conscious state, she would then blurt out words and phrases, as though reliving the ordeal of Ethel's murder. On one such occasion, when detectives were within earshot, Clair had put his hand over his fiancée's mouth, arousing considerable suspicion. The Kinrades explained that Mrs. Kinrade was also close by and, although she knew of Ethel's death, at that point she had not been informed that her daughter had been murdered.

Given the publicity surrounding the case, the presence of reporters from distant cities and the impossibility of squelching gossip, it seems unbelievable that Mrs. Kinrade did not know what was going on.

She was kept away from the inquest for as long as possible and was kept away from the official proceeding on doctor's orders. But when she did finally make an appearance, she seemed extremely calm and composed. And so did Florence, much of the time. But there were astute observers who noticed that Florence seldom looked directly at Crown Attorney George Tate Blackstock when he questioned her, preferring to keep her eyes on the ceiling. Repeatedly, whenever Blackstock pointed out that she was contradicting herself, she reminded him that the she had been terribly frightened at the time. Even more often, she simply collapsed, which forestalled further questions.

One of the most dramatic examples of Florence's fainting spells came during a particularly lengthy examination by Blackstock.

Under careful questioning, Florence had stated that she had "let out an awful yell" the moment she left the house after the murder. She had made absolutely no reference to that before, and in addition, no one in the neighbourhood had heard her.

By this time there were many who believed that Florence was making up huge portions of the story about Ethel's final moments, and that the tramp was a figment of her imagination. Then, when Blackstock asked Florence who killed her sister, she replied firmly, "I do not know."

Blackstock then asked if she realized that, if the tramp was not present, the only people left in the house were her and her sister. "Yes," Florence replied—and then realized the implication of Blackstock's question. He had tacitly suggested she had killed her sister.

Before she said another word, Blackstock dismissed

her. "That will do, Miss Kinrade," he said. But Florence was already reacting to his implied accusation. She called for water and slumped in the witness box. Her fiancé and a private nurse hurried to her assistance. Clair picked her up and carried her out of the room. Just as he passed the coroner, Florence began to rave, "I see the man, I see the man. He will shoot me! He will shoot me! Oh, quick, help!"

Clair and the nurse were followed by Dr. C. K. Clarke, a prominent "alienist," or pioneer psychiatrist, who had previously examined Florence and other family members. He was convinced that she was faking her condition. She had not gone pale during her spell, and when Clarke took her pulse it was completely normal. Clarke then told Florence to sit up and she did so immediately, looking rather smug at the success of her performance.

What was not yet common knowledge was that Clarke had come to the conclusion that there were serious emotional problems in the Kinrade family. Florence, he believed, was a "moral imbecile"—an immature and impulsive psychopath who did not know right from wrong—and her family was using all its wealth and influence to protect her.

Detectives had told reporters that Thomas Kinrade had been extremely helpful in the case. He certainly seemed to be, posting a $1,000 reward for capture of Ethel's murderer and cooperating as much as possible. But, time and time again, the excuse of hysteria was used to keep his wife and daughter away from probing questions. Thomas also moved his family to a hotel in Toronto to keep them out of the limelight and used his wealth and influence to protect them. At one point, he threatened to sue anyone who made slanderous statements about Florence.

After the episode when Florence raved about seeing a man who was going shoot her and it seemed Blackstock was getting too close to the truth, Florence did not return to the inquest. The coroner issued a bench warrant for her arrest in order to force her to appear. Thomas Kinrade hired a lawyer to argue that Blackstock's comment "That will do," effectively concluded Florence's participation in the inquest. In addition, the lawyer questioned the coroner's ability to issue a bench warrant.

In the end, the lawyer lost and Florence was required to return to the inquest. But its findings were inconclusive. There was simply not enough solid evidence to bring the case to trial.

Florence and her family left Canada for the United States and, shortly afterwards, against the wishes of his parents, she and Clair were married in New York City. As a result of the scandal, though, all his hopes of a career as a minister were dashed. Instead, he became a lawyer. Although his parents repeatedly asked him to leave Florence, Clair refused. They had one daughter together before he died in the Spanish flu epidemic of 1918.

Florence returned to the stage and pursued a successful career as a singer.

Officially, the murder of Ethel Kinrade was never solved. But bits of information pieced together over the years, including a 1988 article by *Toronto Star* reporter Frank Jones, present a possible story.

After discovering that Florence was working in vaudeville and engaged to an actor, Thomas Kinrade insisted she return to Canada. Florence needed his financial support and complied. She also broke off the engagement with Jimmie Baum, but apparently kept corresponding with him. In late February 1909, either Ethel or her mother found out about the continued contact. Enraged at her sister, Florence shot Ethel.

The first bullet would have been enough to knock Ethel to the floor, but Florence put three more bullets into her chest at close range, then fired two more into the side of her head.

Whether Mrs. Kinrade was in the house at the time or not, she took control, possibly with the assistance of her husband, and spun a credible story about bothersome tramps. Florence waited until her mother had had enough time to reach the police station and tell her story before giving the alarm.

As for the missing gun, a thorough search of the house and grounds failed to turn up anything. Years later, however, a rusty gun was found in a house that had once been owned by Thomas Kinrade. The weapon was too old and damaged to provide any clues. Still, it is possible that the murder revolver was turned over to Florence's brother Ernest, who was working as a building contractor in Hamilton, and it is not unreasonable to think he might have dropped it into the space between the walls of a house that was undergoing renovations.

Florence Kinrade died in 1977 and is buried in Hollywood, California.

Chapter 5
Annie Robinson: "I Did It for Jessie's Sake"

In the summer of 1909, Reverend Dunlop, a Methodist minister in Warren, Ontario, seventy kilometres west of North Bay, wrote to J. J. Kelso in Toronto. Once a crusading reporter and vocal advocate for child welfare, Kelso was superintendent of the Children's Aid Society of Ontario. Dunlop was concerned about the Robinson family.

James and Annie Robinson owned valuable land along the Canadian Pacific Railway line outside of town. They and their ten children had toiled long and hard to make the farm prosperous, and to a great extent had succeeded. Annie was a pleasant woman and a good mother, who attended

Dunlop's church and, for the most part, the family had been considered quite respectable. But that had changed in recent years, when the two oldest Robinson girls became pregnant out of wedlock. In 1906, sixteen-year-old Ellen had given birth to a little boy, who was still living with the family. Then, in early 1908, it had become apparent that Jessie and her younger sister Ellen were both several months pregnant. One story that circulated around the Northern Ontario community was that the fathers-to-be were railroad workers, but some people hinted at a far more sinister possibility—that James Robinson had impregnated his daughters. More troubling still was that, more than a year after the girls had been apparently pregnant, no one had seen either of the babies. And, by the late spring of 1909, Jessie had been noticeably pregnant again.

Kelso promised to investigate, but when nothing happened Dunlop discussed the matter with local authorities. On August 7, when James and Annie Robinson were in town, James was told by Magistrate E. A. Wright that some questions needed to be answered and that he and Dr. Dixon would visit his farm. James nonchalantly told them to come for a visit—but on the way home, he stopped the rig he was driving and began to beat his wife, stopping only when other travellers approached.

On August 9, Wright and Dixon went out to the Robinson farm and were told that Jessie had given birth to a child on

August 4, but it had died. John, her twenty-one-year-old brother, dug up the tiny body and the doctor brought it back to town for an autopsy. His examination indicated the infant had died of natural causes, but the doctor and the magistrate were still convinced that something was not right at the Robinson farm. Before the day was over they decided to make another trip out to the farm, this time accompanied by Ontario Provincial Constable Boyd.

What the Robinsons had initially told them was that on March 7 of the previous year, 1908, Jessie had given birth to a little boy who died soon after birth. On March 23, Ellen's baby was born, which also died. As the men pressed for details, Annie Robinson became more and more agitated, and finally she confessed that she had smothered both babies. She insisted that, although James had been present in one instance, he had had nothing to do with it.

Annie was arrested early Tuesday, and Boyd and Wright still wanted to talk to James. But he was nowhere to be found. A police officer was posted to watch the property through Tuesday night. At seven on Wednesday morning, James walked into his house, totally undetected by officers of the law, washed his face and asked one of his daughters to pack a lunch for him. He then picked up his Winchester rifle and all the cartridges he could find, told his son John, "They'll never get me alive," and left.

Known locally as an expert bushman, James seemed

to disappear into the wilderness. Armed police officers and an experienced guide, Louis Lamarche, searched for him, while the public was asked to keep an eye out. There were reports of sightings, and rumours that he had gone to Washagami, where he had friends, or southeast to Renfrew County, where he and Annie had married, but days passed without any arrest.

On August 13, Annie was arraigned and charged with murder, but, as the details of her story became known, many agreed with the assessment of newspapers like the *Cobalt Daily Nugget* that James Robinson was "the real criminal." While she awaited trial in jail in Sudbury, her brother Peter Matheson arrived with his wife. Matheson was a Presbyterian minister and was determined to help Annie and her family as best he could. He was not alone in this endeavour, for as details of the tragic events on the farm became known, public sympathy for Annie and her daughters grew.

Annie Matheson was born in Westmeath, Renfrew County, around 1864. Although her parents were poor, they took pains to send their children to school and see to their religious training. At twenty-two, she married James Robinson. "I was fond of him and I loved him," she recalled. They moved to neighbouring Ross Township and were at first very happy. "Jimmie," as Annie called him, "was steady, industrious and very kind to me and the children."

That changed in the early 1890s when James began to

drink heavily. Annie alternately pleaded and scolded, but it did not make much difference. Then, in 1901, they decided to move to "New Ontario," as Northern Ontario was called at the time. Although they worked hard and the farm did well, "there was not much merriment at our home," Annie recalled. Visitors were a rarity, and everyone in the family was "very submissive" to James. None of the children ever questioned his orders.

Around 1904, Annie began to suspect something was very amiss in her household. One night, as she was returning from milking their cows, she saw James summon Ellen to come to him in the bush. Although they were out of sight only a few minutes, Annie instinctively sensed something was wrong. When she questioned Ellen, who was not yet thirteen, the girl would tell her nothing. Jessie, who was a year older, also seemed to be hiding something.

Unable to get an explanation from her daughters, Annie confronted her husband. He reacted angrily, saying, "If you ever mention that to me again I will give you a reason that you won't forget, and a good reason."

Afraid and ashamed, Annie said nothing. Then, in 1906, at the age of sixteen, Ellen gave birth to a baby boy. Annie confronted James, and, after a quarrel, he divided the money he had recently received from the sale of a horse, gave half to his family, and left for Washago. He was gone four months.

It was Christmas when he returned, and, perhaps

moved by the spirit of the season and the love she had once felt for him, Annie took him back. Like many women of the era, she probably did not have much choice. She had a large family to care for and few prospects of employment. Perhaps she hoped four months away from his family had given James time to think about the impact his behaviour had on them. But James had not changed. He continued to molest Ellen and Jessie, as well as their younger sister, Maggie.

Jessie was Annie Robinson's favourite child. "She was kind, affectionate and good to all the smaller children, and a great help to me. But above all she was submissive to her father." She was also frailer than Ellen, and, fearing that a pregnancy would further impair her health, Annie and her son John tried to help Jessie escape from the troubled household. Her trunk was packed and she was on her way to Warren when her father caught up with her and brought her back home.

The birth of Jessie's first child culminated in the tragedy that would bring the Robinson's family secrets into the open. When the little boy was born on March 7, 1908, Jessie was prostrated with shame and guilt. Apparently she had not fully understood the consequences of the sexual relationship with her father. Over and over again, she said to Annie, "Oh, Mother, if this can only be kept hidden. If I had only known this."

Overwhelmed by the situation in the household, her

own inability to stop it and her daughter's tears and shame, Annie did the unthinkable. Unseen by anyone, she put a pile of heavy blankets over the infant and walked away.

Her mind churning with emotion, Annie occupied herself with the endless tasks of an early twentieth-century farm wife. Then, after a while, the realization of what she had done began to sink in. She rushed to the bed, but it was too late. The baby had suffocated. Unable to touch the tiny corpse, Annie waited until James came back to the house that night, then helped him bury it on the property.

Less than three weeks later, Ellen gave birth to another child. Still plagued with guilt over what she had done to Jessie's son, Annie intended to raise the newborn, just as she had Ellen's three-year-old. But James had other ideas. When they were alone with the baby, he told her to kill it.

"Oh, Jimmie, I can't do it," Annie pleaded.

"Yes, you must do it," he insisted. "Do the same with it as you did with the other."

The baby's tiny coffin was buried on top of that of his half-brother.

As Annie awaited trial and the hunt for James continued, it seemed everyone was discussing the case. Most people sympathized with Annie, not only because of the emotional effects of James's actions, but also because both Ellen and Jessie were suffering from post-pregnancy complications. By the twentieth of August, the citizens of Warren and the surrounding area were planning a petition to get Annie out on bail, so that she could at least take care of her children. The consensus, according to the newspaper, was that Annie was almost as much a victim as her daughters, and that her inability to care for her children, including the ailing Ellen and Jessie, was threatening her sanity.

In an unusual partnership, David Laporte, owner of the Globe Hotel in Warren, and Mr. Dunlop, the Methodist minister, looked into the possibility of arranging bail. James may have been one of Laporte's customers, and since Annie herself had blamed heavy drinking for James's aberrant behaviour, the minister might well have shamed Laporte into putting up the funds needed to secure Annie's release. The authorities refused to cooperate, however, and Annie remained in jail.

There was also some speculation that her children would be taken into the custody of the Children's Aid Society, but the presence of her brother and sister-in-law averted that situation. Peter Matheson, may have been "retiring, if not shy" according to the newspaper reports, but he had a keen sense of family and civic duty. In the end, it was he who captured James Robinson.

After leaving his family on August 11, James had walked along the Sturgeon River to North Bay, and then on to Callander. On August 14, using the alias W. Ross, he went to work as a logger, and stayed on the job for four weeks.

On Saturday, September 11, he came to the conclusion that his wife had to have been set free by then and headed back to Warren.

His plan had been to walk into the house as though nothing had happened, but as he approached the place on September 13, he saw a strange woman and hesitated. James waited until everyone had retired, then quietly went to the loft where his sons slept and woke up John. After a lengthy discussion, in which John explained that the woman was Peter Matheson's wife, James took some blankets and went to hide in the barn.

John and his sixteen-year-old brother Tom had already helped their father elude authorities before, resulting in their arrest on August 30 and brief incarceration in the same jail as their mother. Now free, this time John was determined to do the right thing. The next morning, he informed his uncle that James had returned. As they worked together harvesting oats, Peter discussed plans for a capture. John was reluctant, unwilling to seize his father himself, but agreed that if his uncle could disable him temporarily, he would help tie him up.

James stayed out of sight until dinnertime, when he boldly entered the house and sat on a trunk. When Peter asked what he was going to do, James replied that he had been advised to give himself up and that it would be better for him in the long run. Peter concurred. Then James asked for dinner. Concerned that his nieces might also be arrested for aiding and abetting a fugitive, Peter refused to allow them to serve their father, but told his brother-in-law he could help himself.

As he ate the meal, Peter again asked James what he planned to do, and James retorted that he thought he would shoot himself. Assuming his ministerial role, Peter told James that was the coward's way out, and, in addition, it would make him "a prisoner for all eternity" since it would damn his soul to hell. He urged James to face the consequences of his actions.

Although James insisted his wife and daughters had committed far worse crimes than he had, he said he would take the train to Sudbury and turn himself in. But later, when he commented that he could likely elude authorities for twenty years, Peter came to the conclusion that James would never willingly surrender to the police.

After dinner James told his daughters to heat some water and wash his clothes. Again Peter intervened, reminding him of the possible legal consequences if the girls assisted him in any way. At that point, James lost patience and said he still had something to do with the running of his own household. Then he put the water on to boil and told Jessie to come with him to the storehouse where his clean clothes were kept. This Peter absolutely forbade. James was becoming more and more difficult, and, in Peter's opinion, seemed to want to get him and John away from the house. At one point he suggested they start hauling the oats out of the field. Then he went to the storage area where his clean clothes were.

While he was there, Peter fetched a leather strap from the stable. Moments after James returned to the house with a bundle of clothing, Peter lunged at him from behind, pulling him down to the floor. As both men lay face upward, John seized the strap and got it around his father's left wrist. After some struggling, he managed to tie the other hand as well. Meanwhile, James kicked so violently that Peter and John decided to tie his ankles together with a rope. Then they waited until James calmed down, untied his legs, and carted him off to Warren to board a train for Sudbury.

Court proceedings got under way in September. Because there was so much sympathy for Annie and her girls, local lawyers refused to act for the Crown, so a special prosecutor, A. E. H. Creswick, was brought in from Barrie. Annie's lawyer entered a plea of not guilty and arranged for her to be tried separately from James.

Annie's trial began on September 21. She was near collapse as her sister-in-law escorted her to the witness box. Sometimes trembling, often breaking down into pitiful sobs, she recounted her early suspicions and her daughters' unwanted pregnancies. At one point, her lawyer, James Mulligan of Sudbury, asked her why she hadn't written to her mother, who was still alive, or spoken to friends in Warren about James's assaults on their daughters. The only explanation Annie could offer was that she was both ashamed of what was going on in her home and afraid to defy her husband.

When Mulligan asked why she had killed her grandson, Annie broke down completely. After several minutes, she was handed a glass of water, but was trembling so severely she could not lift the glass to her lips. Finally, she responded. "I did it for Jessie's sake, the poor girl. It being my own daughter that was being disgraced and my husband the means of her downfall, it was then I decided to kill it."

But there was no doubt that she suffered terrible remorse over what she had done. "Until today I can hear that poor baby crying," she told the court.

Jessie also gave heart-wrenching testimony, the details of which were too "revolting" for publication in Canadian newspapers. What little information they did print records that Jessie had meekly submitted to her father's demands, demands which had resulted in two pregnancies. Many of those listening to her story were in tears by the time she finished.

Given the huge amount of sympathy the case had engendered, Creswick had to tread carefully. "One can hardly imagine a more horrible, a more terrible state of affairs," he told the jury, adding that everyone sympathized with Annie. "But sympathy doesn't count in the eyes of the law, and you are here to judge this woman according to the evidence given."

Annie Robinson: *"I Did It for Jessie's Sake"*

The trial continued the following day, with evidence presented on the murder of the second baby. When it was time to instruct the jury, Judge Magee made it clear that his sympathy also went out to Annie, but he would adhere to the letter of the law. Bring in a verdict of guilty, he told the jury, but with a strong recommendation of mercy.

Despite the judge's instruction, the members of the jury followed their hearts. Not once, but twice, they rendered verdicts of not guilty. But, each time, Judge Magee sent them back to reconsider, and finally they acquiesced. Annie Robinson was declared guilty of two counts of murder. Sentencing was put off until September 28. In the meantime, a bit of a controversy broke out because of Magee's decision to send the jury back to reconsider their verdicts. Some people questioned the legality of the action, but it was finally made clear that what had been done was perfectly acceptable in law.

When the time for sentencing came, Annie was in tears as she entered the courtroom. She stood in the dock, leaning her elbows on the rail, her face buried in a handkerchief that did nothing to muffle her sobs. Judge Magee was brief and to the point. He made it clear that he wished someone else had to handle this difficult task. He had the greatest sympathy for her, he said, describing her as "a woman of forty-five, broken in mind and body." But she had also been found guilty of "one of the highest crimes in the land" and there was no option but to sentence her to death. While he concurred with the jury's recommendation for mercy, Judge Magee cautioned Annie against building up her hopes of escaping the gallows. Instead, he urged her to spend the next few weeks preparing for eternity. As she stepped down, two constables escorted her from the courtroom, followed closely by her brother Peter.

Because of the rumours about James's mental state, a "lunacy commission" was organized to examine his sanity. That resulted in a slight delay in his trial, but it went ahead after he was deemed mentally competent. Initially, James had been charged with two murders, as well as three counts of incest, three of rape and three of carnal knowledge of a child under fourteen, but the charges had been reduced. Nevertheless, James pleaded not guilty.

Much of the evidence had already been heard at Annie's trial. Things took a slightly new twist, however, when Ellen became too sick to appear in court. The judge transferred proceedings to the Cook and Arthur Hospital so that the jurors could hear her testimony. Annie was also called as a witness, but James's defence attorney objected. First of all, he argued, she was under sentence of death and therefore was legally dead. Secondly, a wife could not testify against her husband. The judge overruled the defence attorney's first argument and skirted the second by forbidding Annie from repeating anything James had said to her. But the statements she had previously given into evidence were corroborated by what John and Ellen had overheard, including the conversation in which James had urged Annie to kill the second baby, just as she had done with the first.

In the meantime, Canadians were protesting Annie's death sentence. By early October, the Toronto Suffrage Association was petitioning for a new trial. Spokesperson Augusta Stowe Gullen refuted criticism that the petition might be seen as condoning the murder of illegitimate children. The daughter of pioneering female physician Emily Stowe dismissed the charges in her usual no-nonsense fashion. "There could be no reasonable doubt of the insanity of a woman under the stress of such circumstances," she told reporters. The Nipissing Women's Christian Temperance Union also protested, although their main focus was to overturn the death sentence, repeating Justice Magee's description of Annie as, "a woman broken in body and mind."

Among those who signed one of the petitions to save Annie from the gallows was James Robinson.

On November 6, it was announced that Annie's death sentence had been overturned. Three days later, she learned that she would serve ten years in Kingston penitentiary. But there were plenty of people who considered even that punishment far too severe. In the end, Annie Robinson served just over eighteen months in prison before being paroled.

Chapter 6
Elizabeth Tilford:
"Honey, You Are Not Going to Die"

On the morning of Thursday, March 28, 1935, Tyrrell Tilford stumbled across the short distance separating his house from that of his parents. As he entered their house at 186 Norwich Avenue in Woodstock, he announced to his parents and sister, "I have come home to die."

For more than a month, Tyrrell had been complaining of burning pains in his stomach. Over the past few weeks, his condition had deteriorated rapidly. He was growing weaker, vomited frequently and was so dizzy he couldn't walk properly. In addition, his tongue looked raw, "as if it had been sliced all over with a knife," according to his elderly mother.

Tyrrell was thirty-five and worked as a teamster. Five years earlier, at the age of thirty, he had married forty-five-year-old Elizabeth Walker. Like Tyrrell, Lizzie had been born in England, where she had married her first husband, Frank Yaxley, at the age of sixteen. According to rumours, she did it on a dare. The marriage did not last long enough for her to seriously regret her decision. Frank died within a couple of years.

Lizzie found solace in the Salvation Army, where she rose to the rank of captain. She also taught Sunday school. Through the Salvation Army she met her second husband, William Walker, who was about six years older. They married in 1911 and had four children.

In 1928, the Walkers immigrated to Canada and settled in Woodstock, Ontario. Like most immigrants, they hoped to find a better life in their adopted country, but time was running out for William. A year after arriving in Canada, he died of a brain tumour and was buried in the Woodstock Baptist Cemetery.

Lizzie struggled along on a widow's pension, augmenting it from time to time by reading tea leaves. Then she met Tyrrell, and, despite the difference in their ages, they married in 1932. Neither of his parents attended the wedding, nor did his brothers, who were told of the marriage just hours before the ceremony. Although the senior Tilfords allowed Tyrrell to build a small house on a corner of their property, they never visited the home their son shared with this new wife and stepchildren. Tyrrell's father, in particular, disapproved of the large difference in the couple's ages.

By 1934, there was more reason for disapproval. According to local gossip, which Tyrrell apparently believed, Lizzie had become involved with another man, William Blake. A widower who owned two farms, Bill Blake was forty-two and had first met Lizzie when one of her teenage sons brought him home to have his tea leaves read. Although Tyrrell complained to both Lizzie and his family about the other man's visits, Blake continued to call at the house when Tyrrell was elsewhere.

With Bill Blake in the picture, Tyrrell became convinced he was being poisoned, and that the burning in his stomach and other symptoms were the result. "She has killed two husbands and I am the third. I'm sure she'll kill no more," he told his mother. He claimed that arsenic was being put in his food, in his water, in his tea, and, at one time, that it had been sprinkled on his tongue. Yet no one confronted Lizzie with the suspicions or complained to the police. Tyrrell did not seek medical help, and he continued to live with his wife despite the growing estrangement between them.

A few hours after he told his family he had come home to die, his sister Annie encountered Lizzie and told her that her mother was taking care of Tyrrell. She also said that she thought he should go to the hospital. Lizzie was infuriated, telling her sister-in-law that Tyrrell had no business taking any medicine or food unless she gave it to him. Then she stamped her foot and said, "He's not going to no hospital. If he is going to die he'll die at home."

On Friday, Tyrrell's mother Mary called a Woodstock drugstore owned by Hutcheson Keith to see if any arsenic had been sent to her son's house. At that time, people often used the poison to eliminate rats, and druggists were required to keep careful records about who purchased arsenic and how much. Someone at the store confirmed that arsenic had been delivered, but "not for weeks and weeks." When she relayed the information to her son, Tyrrell commented, "That's a lie, and a big one."

Dr. Hugh Lindsay was called in. Tyrrell's symptoms were somewhat perplexing, but the doctor suspected influenza, jaundice and myocarditis, an inflammation of the heart. He did not, however, think the young man's life was in danger. In fact, when he called again on Saturday, he told his patient he would be much better by Tuesday or Wednesday. "Why you damn fool," snapped Tyrrell's father James. "The lad's dying now." Tyrrell held the same opinion. "I'll be dead by Tuesday," he told the doctor. He was so convinced that he was dying that he sent for his brother-in-law Walter Allan in order to make out a will. He also sent for Lizzie.

Around eight in the evening, Lizzie was sitting on the bed beside Tyrrell, with various members of his family gathered nearby. "You know, honey," Lizzie said to her husband, "you should not have come here." Tyrrell pushed her away, retorting, "You know, Lizzie, you have been poisoning me." According to James Tilford, Tyrrell's father, the accusation didn't fluster Lizzie one bit. "She sat there bold as a lion," he later recalled.

When Tyrrell said he was dying, Lizzie soothed him. "Honey, you are not going to die." The remark irritated James. "You great bloody cow," he said to his daughter-in-law.

Then Tyrrell said, "Lizzie, you can soon have your man with the two farms, Bill Blake."

Lizzie stood up. "Well, I like that!" she said huffily. Yet, in spite of the accusations, when his brother-in-law Walter arrived, Tyrrell instructed him to draw up a will leaving everything to Lizzie.

Later that night, after everyone had gone to bed, James Tyrrell was disturbed by noises in the kitchen. He got up to find that his son had moved from the bedroom to a couch. Early Sunday morning, he again heard noises. When he went downstairs, he discovered that Tyrrell and Lizzie had gone back to their own house.

On Sunday, Tyrrell's condition deteriorated. At one point he became delusional and thrashed about in the bed. Norman, Lizzie's son, held him down until he became calm. Around two o'clock Monday morning, Tyrrell died. After the news was relayed to his family, some of them dropped by the house. At one point when she was alone with her brother-in-law Tom, Lizzie referred to a prior discussion about the possibility of doing an autopsy. "If your dad is going to have this boy's stomach out," she warned, "it will cost him $3,000 and a public apology in every newspaper in Canada."

The elder Tilford did try to arrange for an autopsy. Dr. Lindsay was consulted, and he, in turn, talked to the Crown Attorney, but the Crown felt there was no need for further investigation. Funeral arrangements went ahead. Tyrrell's body was embalmed, dressed, and then returned to his own home in a casket.

Friends and family called at the house prior to the funeral, but from time to time there was no one with the remains except close family. One evening, when Lizzie was alone with her sister-in-law Agnes, she shared a bizarre secret. Lizzie had removed Tyrrell's body from the casket, taken off his clothing and examined him. She was happy to see that he was wearing underwear, disappointed that the undertaker had cut up the back of his good coat, but, most importantly, was satisfied that there were no signs of an autopsy. "They are not going to put anything over on me," she said. Agnes was shocked.

At the funeral service, Lizzie flung herself over the coffin and cried, "Oh, Tyrrell, why have you gone and left me to face this out alone?" But she had already put some plans in place. A few weeks earlier she had asked questions about their insurance policies, and she also knew, from previous experience, that she would qualify for a widow's pension. But she was still anxious about the possibility of an autopsy. In fact, she was so concerned that she sent her sons William and Norman to the cemetery on the night after the funeral to make sure her husband's grave was undisturbed.

It might have remained undisturbed except that Tyrrell's family made repeated calls to the police station, insisting on an investigation. Finally, the Ontario Provincial Police agreed. Detective Edward D. Hammond was assigned to the case. The first thing he did on arriving in Woodstock was to visit local drugstores to find out who had purchased poison. It wasn't long before he learned that two ounces of arsenic had been delivered to the Tilford home on March 20. The druggist, Hutcheson Keith, clearly recalled that Elizabeth Tilford had phoned in the order, because he recognized her English accent. But when the delivery boy, Victor King, showed up with the arsenic and the "poison book," Elizabeth was not at home. Instead, her daughter Isabella had signed for the delivery. For the sake of consistency, Keith had changed the name on the order.

Hammond then visited the Tilford home and spoke to Isabella. She told him that on the day the arsenic was delivered, her stepfather arrived home before her mother. She immediately turned the package over to him, and Tyrrell asked her not to tell Lizzie that the arsenic had arrived. With a little further investigation, he also learned that, on the day after Tyrrell's death, his brothers Tom and Frank had called on Lizzie and casually mentioned that they had seen a rat outside the house. "We have had no rats around here since we have been here." She also denied that there was any poison in the house.

As far as Hammond was concerned, the whole situation smelled suspicious. He arranged for an exhumation and an autopsy. Tyrrell's heart, liver, right kidney and stomach were removed for analysis. The initial results were inconclusive, so a second autopsy was arranged. Dr. E. R. Frankish, the provincial pathologist, found more than two grains of arsenic in Tyrrell's body, more than enough to kill a man. Lizzie was arrested.

She went to trial in September and was defended free of charge by the law team of Frank Regan and C. W. Bell. Cecil L. Snyder of Toronto handled the prosecution. Various members of Tyrrell's family told the court what they had heard and how the dead man had insisted he was being poisoned. One of Lizzie's acquaintances also related a disturbing story. In 1928, Lily MacDougall's husband had been ill and very irritable. Lizzie, who had done some practical nursing back in England, suggested she prepare a dish of potatoes and one of carrots and lace it with salts of lemon, a poisonous crystalline substance used in removing ink stains.. "You'll soon get rid of him," she told Lily. Lizzie's lawyer suggested that it had been a joke, but Mrs. MacDougall said she took the matter so seriously she had mentioned it to her mother.

Tyrrell's physical state was a matter of serious concern. According to his mother, he had been in good health all his life, except for an operation on his ear at the age of seven. There was some speculation that a plate had been put into his head, infection had developed, and this had led to various complications. But Mary Tilford said she had never heard about her son having a plate in his head, and apparently no one had looked for it in either autopsy. The court heard Dr. Lindsay testify that the official cause of death was myocarditis, influenza and catarrhal jaundice. Dr. Lindsay also indicated that if Tyrrell had been suffering from uremia because of kidney failure, he might have experienced paranoid delusions and believed someone was trying to kill him.

One theory that was presented was that Tyrrell had been suffering from a strangulated hernia. According to the defence, he had been scheduled for an operation to cure the problem. Dr. Frankish, the expert medical witness who had conducted the second autopsy, said there was absolutely no evidence to suggest that a strangulated hernia had caused Tyrrell's death.

Then, as now, the testimony of medical experts carried considerable weight. But there were problems with the procedure. All the organs removed from Tyrrell's body had been put together in one container, which meant that the kidney, heart and liver may have been contaminated by the contents of the stomach. The first, inconclusive autopsy had been carried out by Professor Joslyn Rogers, a chemist. Because he was not a pathologist, he had not examined the interior of the heart to look for myocarditis that might have killed Tyrrell. Dr. Frankish was also handicapped when he did the second autopsy because he was not given the organs to examine. In addition, under questioning by one of Lizzie's lawyers, he admitted that he had dealt with only two cases of murder by arsenic in his entire career, and one case of suicide by arsenic.

One of the theories C. W. Bell was building was that Tyrrell had become depressed because of his physical condition and decided to kill himself. Why had he not told Dr. Lindsay that he thought he was being poisoned? Why had he not left the house he shared with Lizzie, or at least asked one of his brothers to take him out of there? How could he, on one occasion, state that Lizzie was doing everything she could for him, and then accuse her of poisoning him? His behaviour was often illogical, and sometimes delusional. At one point he had claimed that someone was looking at him from behind the curtains that covered his bedroom door, but no one was there. And the story that "they" had poured poison on his tongue was a "fantastic tale."

Bell did not call any witnesses for the defence, not even his client. Quite possibly he was concerned that Lizzie would harm her case if she took the stand. She was heavyset and not particularly attractive, her marriage to a man fifteen years younger than herself was considered scandalous—and then there were the rumours of a relationship with Bill Blake. Added to this was Lizzie's habit of speaking her mind in the middle of the proceedings. When Cecil Snyder asked why the prisoner had sent her two sons to check on Tyrrell's grave, Lizzie shouted, "She did not!" Judge Kingstone immediately ordered Bell to keep his client quiet.

Instead of calling witnesses, Bell chose to undermine prosecution witnesses and present an alternative explanation of events to the jury. As far as he was concerned, there was no proof that Lizzie had given her husband poison. Annie, Tyrrell's sister, had stated that Lizzie had tried to give him a capsule which she claimed Dr. Lindsay had prescribed, but Tyrrell had brought it back up. Lizzie had then broken open the capsule and tossed it into the stove. Bell also argued that those who poison worked in the dark. If Lizzie intended to kill her husband, why would she have openly ordered arsenic from the druggist? And what did she have to gain? There was no significant amount of insurance money, and the house she lived in was on property belonging to her in-laws.

In his closing statements, Bell also warned jurors about the consequences a guilty verdict might have. He referred to another case he had handled, in which his client had been convicted of a serious crime and sent to prison. Then another man confessed. "Had that been a capital case and a verdict returned by the jury, that man would now have been five months under ground."

In his instructions to the jury, the Justice Kingstone urged the members to make up their own minds about Lizzie's behaviour and possible guilt. But he did draw attention to the fact that she had taken her husband's body out of the casket. "What do you think of a woman who would do that, gentlemen? I think it is extraordinary behaviour, to put it mildly. Was it for the purpose of satisfying herself whether some authority had been making an investigation? It may have been of no significance, gentlemen, but you have got to consider it."

The jury withdrew. Lizzie had occasionally shown signs of anxiety during her trial, but at this point, the tension proved overwhelming. She fainted and had to be carried to a nearby anteroom and placed on a table until she regained consciousness. It took six hours for the jury to reach a verdict. When they returned to court, they announced that they had found Elizabeth Tilford guilty of murder. She was immediately sentenced to hang on December 17.

Her lawyers launched an appeal. On December 9, Cabinet decided to let the sentence stand. Their decision was announced a week later.

Lizzie took comfort in religion and remained relatively composed, except when discussing her children. Her two young children, Isabella and Johnny, had been sent to live with relatives in Detroit in order to protect them from hearing the details of the approaching execution.

On December 16, Lizzie's lawyer, Frank Regan, released a statement that she had written. "It is better to go innocent than to stay here guilty," it began. "Death is only a crossing over. I have no fear, for I go to meet my Maker, innocent."

Shortly before 1 a.m. on December 17, a small group emerged from the doorway leading to the jail yard. Lizzie was dressed entirely in black. She was very pale, her head bowed, and she moved forward with a guard on each side of her. Nearby, a Reverend Dixon read from the Bible.

Slowly and steadily, Lizzie mounted the thirteen steps to the scaffold and, without another word, went to meet her maker.

Her older sons had arranged for Lizzie to be laid to rest beside their father. The funeral took place in Woodstock's Baptist Cemetery at 2:30 a.m., by flashlight, with Reverend Dixon officiating. None of her family attended. The only witnesses were the clergyman, the matron and a handful of newspaper reporters.

Chapter 7

Elizabeth Popovich: "Can't I Kiss My Daughters Goodbye?"

On September 13, 1946, Elizabeth Popovich and her husband George were found guilty of the murder of Louis Nato. Moments later, Justice W. Schroeder sentenced the couple to hang at the Welland County jail on November 12.

The words were barely out of his mouth when Elizabeth leaned heavily against her husband, her arms around his neck. Three rows behind them, Elizabeth's two daughters, eighteen-year-old Florence and thirteen-year-old Helen, screamed, "Oh no, no, no!" They sobbed, rising from their seats and trying to reach their mother. Two Ontario Provincial Police officers held them back as their stepfather was handcuffed and led from the courtroom. Then, as Elizabeth stepped down from the prisoner's dock, she collapsed. A police matron held her up, and after a moment or two she partially recovered, looked directly at Thorold Chief of Police Dennis Harold and cried, "Can't I kiss my daughters goodbye?"

Harold shook his head. It was not allowed. "Let me kiss my children goodbye before you take me away," Elizabeth pleaded. "Let me kiss my children goodbye, my God!" She was escorted out of the courtroom as her daughters were comforted by friends.

Concern over the welfare of her three daughters had played a small part in the path that was now leading Elizabeth Popovich to the gallows. After her first husband died, Elizabeth Johnson had struggled to support her family. One way she earned money was by working in a combined grocery store and café owned by Louis Nato, a Yugoslavian immigrant about twelve years her senior. The relationship went well beyond work. Elizabeth became Nato's "housekeeper," the euphemistic term for mistress. He gave her $1,000 to pay off her debts and buy clothing for her children. He also allowed her to use his car whenever she needed it.

Their relationship lasted for a couple of years, around 1943 and 1944, and then Elizabeth became involved with a Polish immigrant, George Popovich. Soon they were telling friends and acquaintances in the small Niagara peninsula community of Thorold South that they were planning to marry. Nato was not happy when he heard the news. On several occasions, he asked Chief of Police Dennis Harold to intervene, to tell Elizabeth not to marry George. Harold passed the message on to Elizabeth, but she had no intention of changing her plans. "I delivered Nato's message twice," Harold would testify at the murder trail, "but she said that she would marry George because Nato hadn't treated her right."

The marriage went ahead as planned but the trio remained involved to some extent. Then, at 3 a.m. on June 16, Louis Nato staggered into the home of a friend, Helen Weiser. He was wearing a sweater and long underwear, and he had been badly beaten. His face and neck were bruised, his ribs broken, and ropes were attached to his hands and feet. In addition, his trousers had been ripped off, his wallet emptied, and his car stolen.

Nato wanted to call a taxi, but Mrs. Weiser did not own a phone. She gave him a glass of water, wiped some of the blood from his face, and sent him on his way. Around three thirty he stumbled into a store owned by a John Tychynski. Quickly assessing his friend's condition, Tychynski told Nato to lie down while he called the police.

When Dennis Harold questioned him, Nato refused to reveal any information, except the obvious fact that he had been attacked. Harold got the impression that it was a personal matter, one that Nato preferred to handle himself. Postponing serious questioning for another time, Harold focused on the most urgent matter at hand, getting Nato medical treatment. After Nick Bougay, another local resident, provided some first aid, Nato was taken to Maplehurst Hospital, a privately run establishment where he was treated by Dr. W. H. McMillan. Aside from bruises and broken ribs, Nato had a fractured skull. At first, it seemed he would recover, but after a couple of days his condition deteriorated. Sensing what was happening, the injured man spoke of his imminent death to both Dr. McMillan and to Florence Stevenson, the owner of the hospital. For the first time, he revealed the details of what had taken place in the early morning hours of June 17.

"I know who did this to me," he told Dr. McMillan. "Liz Johnson and that man of hers, Popovich. They did this to me and took my money." He repeated the same story to Florence Stevenson.

According to Nato, Elizabeth and George Popovich had showed up at his house and asked him to drive them somewhere. He agreed, and was directed to a secluded rural road. Once there, the couple attacked him, dragging him from the car, punching and kicking him in the face and head until he passed out. When he regained consciousness, he was lying in a ditch. His trousers had been ripped off and tossed aside, $180 removed from his wallet, his watch and car stolen.

Soon after he told Stevenson and McMillan the details of his attack, Louis Nato slipped into a coma. He was transferred to St. Catharines General Hospital, where he died on June 21.

Armed with Nato's deathbed statement, Ontario Provincial Police Inspector George MacKay pursued the investigation. George Popovich said the story was ridiculous. He had his own car, so he did not need Louis Nato or anyone else to drive him around. He and Elizabeth said they had been nowhere near the scene. They had left their house at 8:45 p.m. on July 16 and went to visit a friend, taxi-driver John Sewich, in Welland. They spent the next several hours chatting with Sewich, until leaving around two in the morning on Monday in order to get something to eat at a restaurant in Crowland. When they found the restaurant closed, they returned to Welland, ate at a restaurant on King Street, and reached their house in Thorold South by three o'clock.

Elizabeth's daughter Florence Johnson backed up the story. She told Inspector MacKay that she had heard her mother and stepfather return at the time they said. But the Popoviches' story started to crumble as the investigation proceeded.

Charles Manning, who worked at the Ontario Paper Mill close to Nato's residence, recalled seeing a man and a woman near Nato's place around one thirty in the morning on July 17. A little while later, he saw Nato's car driving away, with Nato at the wheel and the couple in the back seat. But the real clincher was evidence discovered in Nato's car, which was found abandoned on a side street. Inside was a button from a woman's coat, still attached by some thread to a bit of fabric. Police matched the button and fabric to a coat belonging to Elizabeth Popovich.

Elizabeth and George were arrested in early July and held in the Welland jail until the fall assizes. Their trial began on September 10, with Justice W. Schroeder presiding. C. P. Hope handled the case for the Crown, while Elizabeth and George were defended by a lawyer from Niagara Falls, Wendall Musgrove, K. C. To pay for his services, Elizabeth and George sold their bungalow for $800.

Musgrove's case rested on the Popoviches' contention that Nato had framed them in revenge for Elizabeth's rejection. Hope described their explanation as "pure, utter nonsense."

He also undermined the testimony of Florence Johnson, who admitted on the witness stand that she had lied to Inspector MacKay during her initial questioning. Asked to explain her behaviour, the pretty brunette said, "Well I didn't have to tell him everything, did I? Everything I did tell him he didn't believe." She admitted she had got up to talk to her mother after her return home in the wee small hours of June 17, but had no idea what time it was.

Florence was not the only witness whose account of events was undermined by Hope. Under careful questioning, he destroyed the credibility of both cabdriver John Sewich and another man, George Koucar, who claimed he had talked to the Popoviches at two o'clock on the morning of the crime. The lack of a believable alibi, weighed with the button found in Nato's car, Manning's eyewitness account and Nato's deathbed statement, tipped the balance against the Popoviches.

After the Crown and defence attorneys made their closing statements, Justice Schroeder addressed the jury. He spent two hours reviewing the evidence and explaining the workings of the law. While the jury had the option of finding the couple guilty of murder or of manslaughter, or of acquitting them of the crime, he made it clear that a verdict of manslaughter would not be appropriate. The Popoviches had been charged with murder and, the judge stated, "I can find no evidence to justify a reduction of this charge."

After one hour and fifty minutes of jury deliberation, the Popoviches were sentenced to hang. It was the first time in eighty-four years that a husband and wife had received that sentence in Ontario—it had not happened since 1862, when Mary and James Aylward had been sentenced to be hanged in Belleville for the death of a neighbour.

Before the day was out, Wendall Musgrove was talking about an appeal. George had suddenly announced to Justice Schroeder, after hearing the jury's verdict, that he had two more witnesses; and apparently Musgrove did explore that aspect before abandoning it. Instead, the Popoviches would change their story. Both of them signed an affidavit stating that they had committed perjury during the trial and that they wanted to revise their testimony. According to their new version of events, George had caught Elizabeth and Louis Nato alone in Nato's car and a fight had broken out. Nato had been beaten to "teach him a lesson."

Nobody was buying it, especially in light of Charles Manning's testimony that he had seen a couple outside Nato's home on the night in question, and later had watched them drive away in the back of Nato's car. The November 12 execution date was postponed to give the government time to consider the appeal, but in the end that only delayed the inevitable. On December 4, word came from Ottawa that the execution would go ahead the following day.

Construction of the gallows had already begun. From their cells in the nineteenth-century Welland jail, Elizabeth and George heard the hammers making lumber into an instrument of death, close to one of the seven-metre walls surrounding the jail yard. The wall was topped by electric lights that would illuminate the area.

Prison officials began the death watch. Three matrons, working eight hours each, kept a close eye on Elizabeth. A special guard was posted outside George's door.

There were last minute visitors, including thirteen-year-old Helen Johnson, who saw her mother on the afternoon of December 3. Florence was working, and could not get away. A third sister, according to newspaper reports, had gone to the United States in order to escape the pressure of the situation.

For weeks, George had refused to shave. On the night before his execution, he asked for a barber. Elizabeth asked for a hairdresser, who set her dark hair in fashionable curls. But prison officials told reporters that last requests, including special meals, were no longer accommodated. Elizabeth's brother, who refused to give his name to the press, in order to protect his family, said he had come to Welland from Hamilton, only to arrive just minutes after 10 p.m. on December 4. Regulations forbade visitors after that hour had struck, and even though Reverend Harvey G. Forster of the Thorold South United Church tried to intercede, the officials were adamant. All Elizabeth's brother could do was to ask someone to let Elizabeth know that he was there.

"God bless him," Elizabeth said when she learned of his presence. Her brother broke into tears when he heard her response.

Officials also denied a last request for Elizabeth and George to be alone together for a few moments.

Earlier on December 4, a small crowd had gathered on Main Street outside the jail. Most were younger people. Elizabeth could watch them from her cell window, as she looked to see if her thirteen-year-old daughter Helen was among them. Helen apparently was not. According to one newspaper report, she and her sister were in a car, cruising around the area, but that may have been a rumour started by someone in the crowd outside the jail.

The precise time of the execution was left up to the hangman. He chose to deal with the deathly business as early as possible on the morning of December 5. At 12:15 a.m., George and Elizabeth were summoned from their cells. They hugged and kissed each other and then George proceeded to the jail yard, accompanied by Reverend Forster, who had officiated at George and Elizabeth's marriage. As the minister intoned the Lord's Prayer, George climbed the steps of the gallows and was launched into eternity.

Forty-five minutes later, it was Elizabeth's turn. Wearing her favourite black dress, seemingly more controlled than George had been, she walked the short distance to the gallows to the sound of the Lord's Prayer. Poised on the scaffold just before the trap door was sprung, she called out to the assembled officials, "God bless you all."

For years, it had been customary to post an official notice of execution on the door of Canadian jails. This time, there was no notice. Police officers who had witnessed the executions stepped outside and quietly informed some people in the crowd. Word quickly spread as the earthly remains of Elizabeth and George Popovich were quietly moved to Woodlawn Cemetery, where they were interred side by side.

Chapter 8
Evelyn Dick: "I Don't Know Anything About It"

March 16, 1946 was a mild day in the Hamilton area. Although winter was still holding on, spring was in the air. It was a Saturday, and for a group of pre-teen kids, it seemed like a great day for a hike to Albion Falls, a popular picnic spot on the escarpment. The outing turned into a bigger adventure than anticipated. As they explored the area near the falls they made a grisly discovery: a human torso, clad in the remnants of a suit of long underwear.

Although a few other items of clothing were also found, in the first hours of their investigation the police were hampered by lack of information about the victim. But Hamilton city pathologist Dr. William J. Deadman was able to piece together a number of clues. The cause of death was uncertain. Although the victim had been shot, Dr. Deadman speculated that a head injury might have killed him. The dead man was probably about forty, well built, fair-haired and about five feet ten inches tall. He had a congenital cyst on his buttocks that probably made walking difficult. In addition, there was evidence that the man had been paralyzed at some point in his life.

It was not much to go on, but it was enough to raise concerns in at least one Hamilton household. On Monday, March 18, Alexander Kammerer reported that his cousin had been missing for several days. John Dick was a streetcar conductor with the Hamilton Street Railway (HSR). He had been married the previous October but, after separating from his wife, had gone to live with the Kammerers. On March 6, the last time Alexander had seen John, he was going downtown to take care of some business. When he failed to return, Kammerer assumed John had gone back to his wife, or perhaps had returned to his family in Beamsville. What puzzled him was that his usually dependable cousin had not called to tell him where he was.

The Kammerers were Mennonites, somewhat shy and retiring and hesitant to involve the police in what might have been a private family matter. They did contact John's wife, Evelyn, but she reported she had not heard from him.

Kammerer's description seemed to fit that of the mysterious torso. The next day, identification was confirmed by John Dick's brothers-in-law, John and Jacob Wahl. From Jacob, police learned some of the details of a sordid domestic drama. Others were added following interviews with Dick's family and co-workers.

John Dick was a Russian-born Mennonite whose family had settled in Beamsville, a farming community in the Niagara peninsula. Handsome and easy-going, he lived a relatively quiet life. He did not drink heavily or gamble, although he tended to spend too much on cars. He also had problems managing money and frequently borrowed cash from the women he dated.

In September 1945, John started seeing twenty-four-year-old Evelyn White, the daughter of a co-worker, Donald MacLean. Evelyn was dark-haired, dark-eyed, always well dressed and very attractive. The mother of a four-year-old daughter, Evelyn told John that she was the widow of a naval officer who had been killed during the Second World War. After a few weeks of dating, John and Evelyn were married. Almost immediately, their relationship took a turn for the worse.

At the time of the wedding, Evelyn was living in an apartment on James Street South, along with her mother and daughter. John expected to move into the apartment after the wedding, but Evelyn told him it was too small. He would have to stay at his boarding house near Emerald and Cannon

Streets until they could afford to buy a house.

John was a rather unsophisticated fellow, but Evelyn's behaviour made him suspicious. He decided to keep an eye on her. Five nights after the wedding, as he waited in the shadows outside Evelyn's apartment, he saw his wife coming home with another man. Bill Bohozuk was a steelworker whom Evelyn had been seeing for six months prior to her marriage, and whom she continued to date.

John was furious. More maddening revelations followed. Evelyn was not a widow, as she had claimed. She had never been married. She was, according to her own mother, a "social prostitute," a party-girl who exchanged sexual favours for furs, jewellery and other gifts. She had rented the apartment on James Street to entertain her men friends, and, as his new mother-in-law told him, one of the reasons Evelyn did not want John living there was that he would be in the way.

John also discovered that Evelyn had been pregnant three times between 1940 and 1944. As well as Heather, her first child, she had given birth to a stillborn daughter and to a son, Peter David White. At the time of his birth in September 1944, Evelyn had been living with her parents on Rosslyn Avenue. After her father told her that one child in the house was enough, Evelyn said she had given the baby up for adoption.

In spite of his wife's unconventional lifestyle, John wanted to make the union work. He supported Evelyn's decision to buy a house on Carrick Street and they moved there on October 31. Just who provided the money for the down payment is not clear. John told relatives he had provided $1,300, but Evelyn claimed he did not have the money and that she had made the down payment. What was clear was that the deed was in Evelyn's name. Again, John was furious. He kept badgering his wife to put his name on the deed.

Evelyn and John fought constantly about money. There were other strains on the marriage, as well. When John asked what was in a locked suitcase and a trunk in the attic of their new house, Evelyn told him they were full of some of her school things and really none of his business. Alexandra MacLean, Evelyn's mother, never left the two of them alone and made it very apparent that she disliked her new son-in-law. Evelyn's father was even more hostile. Knowing that he would disapprove of the marriage, Evelyn had kept the news from him for two weeks. When Donald MacLean learned from a co-worker that his daughter had married "the damned Russian" he was outraged. After the two men exchanged angry words at work, other HSR employees told John to watch his back. MacLean was a dangerous man.

Unfortunately, John Dick did not understand the meaning of discretion. He told co-workers and family about his problems with Evelyn and her parents. Worse, after Evelyn revealed that her father had been stealing money from the HSR for years, John let MacLean know he was in on the secret. Meanwhile, John had also angered Bill Bohozuk, who threatened to "get him." By February, John was unable to tolerate the situation any longer and moved in with his cousin Alexander Kammerer.

On February 28, John attended his grandmother's funeral in Beamsville. On March 6, he was seen having a meal in a downtown restaurant. That was the last anyone knew of his whereabouts until the Wahls identified his body.

Inspector Charles W. Wood of the Ontario Provincial Police Criminal Investigation Branch was put in charge of the case. Given all the problems John had experienced with his wife, it seemed logical to pay a call at Carrick Avenue. Evelyn, her parents and daughter were having dinner when Wood arrived. He started by mentioning the newspaper stories about the torso that had been found on the mountain. Evelyn said nothing, her face devoid of all emotion. Then Wood dropped a bombshell. "That torso has been identified as the body of your husband."

"Don't look at me!" Evelyn snapped. "I don't know anything about it."

Wood thought otherwise and advised Evelyn he was taking her in for questioning. Donald MacLean asked if he could accompany his daughter to the station and was given permission. He waited for several hours while Evelyn was being interrogated, then left her alone with the police.

Meanwhile, the house at Carrick Avenue was being

searched. Inside a zippered bag in the attic policemen found the remains of an infant, encased in concrete. The body, it was later discovered, was that of Evelyn's son Peter, who she claimed she had given up for adoption.

Further investigation of the house on Carrick Avenue and of Evelyn's parents' house on Rosslyn turned up remnants of burned human bones and a number of items of clothing belonging to an HSR employee. A bloody ticket punch was found in the pocket of a sealskin coat belonging to Evelyn's mother. Investigation also led to a Packard that Evelyn had once owned but had sold to garage owner William Landeg. On March 6, Evelyn had come back to borrow the car. When she returned it several hours later, the seat covers and a blanket were missing. There was also a pool of blood on the front seat. Evelyn told Landeg that her daughter had been in an accident, and she later replaced the seat covers and blanket. But a bloodstained tie was found in the back seat and the blood in the front seat was the same type as John Dick's. Acting on this evidence and information gathered from various sources, police charged Evelyn, her parents and Bill Bohozuk with the murder of John Dick. Evelyn and Bohozuk were also charged in the death of her infant son, while Donald MacLean was charged with stealing thousands of dollars from the Hamilton Street Railway.

At her first court appearance, Evelyn looked strained, pale and withdrawn. By the time she went to trial in October she had recovered her poise and seemed to enjoy being the focus of attention. Despite her incarceration, she was beautifully groomed every day in court. Her hair was carefully coiffed by a fellow prisoner who happened to be a hairdresser, and her lipstick and nail polish were carefully matched. Most of the time she appeared quite cheerful, smiling at the jurors, the lawyers on both sides, courtroom staff, reporters and spectators. Usually they smiled back. Along with exuding a powerful sexual attraction that most men found irresistible, Evelyn was childishly eager to please. The stark contrast between this pretty, pleasant woman and the ghastly murders of which she was accused added a fascinating angle to the proceedings.

Although Evelyn, her father and Bohozuk had been charged together, Evelyn's defence attorneys moved to have her tried separately. Day after day she sat in the courtroom, carefully taking notes as witnesses took the stand, watching them closely as they spoke. When her mother entered the witness box, she dropped her gaze to the paper and kept it there through most of the testimony.

By this time, the public was intimately familiar with the dysfunctional nature of Evelyn's family. Her Scottish-immigrant parents had a stormy marriage, marked by frequent separations. Donald drank heavily, a habit that thoroughly annoyed Alexandra, who was deeply religious but also had a terrible temper. Caught between her two battling parents, Evelyn learned how to please people, but also how to manipulate them to get what she wanted.

Shortly before taking the stand, Alexandra MacLean apparently struck a deal with the Crown attorney. She would testify against her daughter in exchange for immunity. Her story was straightforward. She described Evelyn's prolonged absence on March 6, a failed attempt to hide the Packard in the garage behind the house on Carrick Avenue and an argument between the two of them. Two days later, she told the court, she took her granddaughter to Sherman Avenue to watch the streetcars pass. This was John Dick's regular route, and Heather enjoyed waving to her new stepfather. But John was not on the car that day. She returned to the house and told her daughter that John wasn't working. Evelyn replied that she wouldn't see him again. When Alexandra asked if something had happened to him, Evelyn hissed, "John Dick is dead and you keep your mouth shut!"

Alexandra also testified that her husband had a revolver and ammunition, as well as a large knife with a broad blade that he used for cutting meat for his dog.

Evelyn's version of the events was wildly imaginative. According to her story, a well-dressed Italian man had come to the house looking for John. The man told her that John was breaking up the man's marriage and he wanted him to stop. Shortly after John disappeared, she received a phone call. It was the same man, telling her that the gang had caught up with her husband. He also insisted on meeting her and gave her directions to the rendezvous. Evelyn borrowed the Packard from Bill Landeg and followed the man's instructions. When he climbed into her car, he was carrying a heavy package. He instructed her to drive up the escarpment and to stop at a bend in the road. Then he told her to help him and pulled John's torso from the bag. At the sight, Evelyn vomited, so the man carried his ghastly burden to the edge of the escarpment alone and tossed it over. As they drove back to the city, he tossed the bag and a shirt out of the window.

Perhaps Evelyn might have convinced the jury that her story was true, but she made several crucial mistakes. One of the most serious was visiting Hamilton's Central Police Station on March 12. According to Detective John Freeborn, when he saw the attractive young woman enter the station, he asked what he could do. Evelyn responded by asking if John Dick had been arrested. Freeborn checked the records and reported that no person of that name was in custody. Then he asked, "If he was arrested or there was a warrant out for him, what would the charge be? Non-support?"

"No," Evelyn replied, "It would be running away with money and tickets belonging to the Hamilton Street Railway." Then she left the station.

Evelyn's alleged ride along the escarpment, as well as the fact that HSR tickets and money had been found in her father's house, made her attempt to present herself as a worried wife ridiculous. If John had really been killed by gang members or by a jealous husband, Evelyn knew about his murder four days *before* her visit to the police. Why would she pretend he was missing if she knew differently?

The jury found Evelyn Dick guilty of murder. The judge ordered her to stand and asked if she had anything to say. "I want my case appealed," she told the court. The judge made a note, then pronounced the death sentence. Her execution was scheduled for January 7, 1947.

At first it seemed Evelyn would collapse from the strain. But she pulled herself together, smiling at her defence lawyers as she was led from the room. And she won her appeal. At her second trial, which began in February 1947, she was acquitted.

In the meantime, Donald MacLean was found guilty as an accessory after the fact in John Dick's murder. He was sentenced to five years in prison, to run concurrently with a five-year term for stealing $250,000 from the Hamilton Street Railway.

In March 1947, Evelyn and Bill Bohozuk went to trial for the murder of baby Peter. Bohozuk was cleared, but Evelyn was found guilty of manslaughter. Prior to sentencing, her lawyer, J. J. Robinette, called Hamilton psychiatrist Robert Alexander Finlayson to the stand. According to Dr. Finlayson, Evelyn had the mental capacity of a thirteen-year-old. Her vocabulary was limited, as was her ability to reason and to make sound judgements, but her excellent memory helped compensate for some of her shortcomings. Finlayson blamed her problems on the insecurity of her childhood and said it was possible she could develop normally in future circumstances.

Judge LeBel concluded that prison would provide more security and support for Evelyn than she had experienced in the past. He sentenced her to life imprisonment in Kingston Penitentiary.

Evelyn remained in prison until 1958, when she was released on parole. Recognizing that her notoriety would make it next to impossible for her to lead a normal life, authorities arranged for her to assume a new identity. Although she was still required to report to police and prison authorities as long as she remained on parole, her new name became a closely guarded secret.

There were rumours, however, and plenty of them. Instead of fading into obscurity, Evelyn Dick became a Hamilton legend. Over the years, various stories emerged. Some people said she was a sales clerk working in an east-end Hamilton shopping mall. Other reports claimed that she had been treated at a mental hospital. In 1987, when a reclusive, elderly couple were accidentally asphyxiated by stove fumes in Binbrook, south of Hamilton, neighbours reported long-held suspicions that the woman was none other than Evelyn Dick.

Most compelling of all was the story told by Mary Louise Lynch, who served for many years on the National Parole Board and later became friendly with Evelyn. According to Lynch, the psychiatric report on Evelyn's limited mental capacity was wrong—she was actually very clever. She emerged as a well-liked natural leader during her time in the penitentiary. After her release, she started a successful business, then married a wealthy man and enjoyed the life to which she had always aspired. At one point she was briefly reunited with her daughter Heather, by this time a married woman with a daughter of her own. Although she was delighted to see Heather and her granddaughter, Evelyn refused to divulge any information about her alias.

In 1985, when Evelyn was 65, she was granted a pardon. Her file was permanently sealed.

Her whereabouts remain a mystery.

Acknowledgements

Quoted material used in this book was drawn from the following published sources:

Bathurst Courier and Ottawa General Advertiser; Cobalt Daily Nugget; Hamilton Spectator; Hamilton Times; Hamilton Herald; Moodie, Susanna, *Life in the Clearings Versus the Bush,* 1853; *Napanee Beaver; Napanee Standard; Perth Courier; Sarnia Observer; Toronto British Colonist; Toronto Daily Mail; Toronto Star; The Trials of James McDermott and Grace Marks at Toronto, Upper Canada, November 3rd and 4th, 1843, for the murder of Thomas Kinnear, esquire and his housekeeper Nancy Montgomery.* Toronto: *Star and Transcript,* 1843; *Woodstock Sentinel Review.*

Thanks go to the many people who have heard my presentation on "Deadly Women of Ontario" and shared their own tales of deadly women, and to those who have helped in locating material for the book, including: Donna Macleod, Mary Rae Shantz and Alan Walker, Toronto Reference Library; Margaret Houghton and Wendy Watson, Hamilton Public Library Special Collections; Anne Ashton, Dana Johnson and Laurie McBeth, Heritage Sarnia-Lambton Museums; Adam

Pollard, Woodstock Museum National Heritage Site; John Rochon, Sarnia; Robert Tremain, Heritage Sarnia-Lambton Museums; Serge Barbe, City of Ottawa Archives; Brigitte Pollock, Historical Society of Ottawa ; Shelley Respondek, Lennox and Addington Museum and Archives; Chris Packman, Woodstock; Sandra Enskat, Special Collections, St. Catharines Public Library; Jim Fortin, City of Greater Sudbury Heritage Museum; Paul Walker, North Bay Public Library; Penny Morningstar and Jodi Welland Historical Museum; Cindy Robidas, Markstay Warren Public Library.

Special thanks go to Jennifer Bunting, former archivist, County of Lennox & Addington Museum and Archives, who provided the background information and transcripts on the Eleanor Navin case.

Finally, extra special thanks go to my editor, Laurie Miller, both for his attention to detail and for his thoughtful and considerate approach to editing.

Further Reading

Atwood, Margaret. *Alias Grace*. Toronto: McClelland and Stewart, 1996.

Campbell, Marjorie Freeman. *Torso: The Evelyn Dick Case*. Toronto: Macmillan of Canada, 1974.

MacDonald, Cheryl. *Deadly Women of Ontario: Murderous Tales of Deceit and Treachery*, 2nd ed. Toronto: James Lorimer and Company Limited, 2010.

———. *Who Killed George? The Ordeal of Olive Sternaman*. Toronto: Natural Heritage Books, 1994.

About the Author

Cheryl MacDonald has been writing about Canadian history for more than thirty years. A long-time resident of Nanticoke, Ontario, she is a full-time writer and historian whose weekly history column appears in the *Simcoe Times-Reformer*. Her historical articles have appeared in *The Beaver*, *Maclean's*, the *Hamilton Spectator* and *The Old Farmer's Almanac*. Cheryl has written, co-authored or edited nearly forty books on Canadian and Ontario history, including Amazing Stories titles *Deadly Women of Ontario*, *Murder!* and *Great Canadian Imposters*. A member of both Professional Writers of Canada and Crime Writers of Canada, Cheryl can be reached through her website, www.heronwoodent.ca.

Index